Cross Stitch
Greeting Cards

Cross Stitch Greeting Cards

OVER 50 DESIGNS FOR EVERY OCCASION

Lynda Burgess
and
Julia Tidmarsh

HAMLYN

CROSS STITCH GREETING CARDS

Lynda Burgess and Julia Tidmarsh

First published in 1997 by Hamlyn
an imprint of Reed Consumer Books Limited
Michelin House, 81 Fulham Road
London, SW3 6RB
and Auckland, Melbourne, Singapore and Toronto

Publishing Director LAURA BAMFORD

Executive Editor SIMON TUITE
Project Editor KATIE COWAN
Editor CAROLINE BINGHAM

Art Director KEITH MARTIN
Executive Art Editor MARK STEVENS
Art Editor LISA TAI

Special Photography by LAURA WICKENDEN
Photograph on page 104-5 by DEBI TRELOAR
Illustrations by LESLEY WAKERLY

Production JOSEPHINE ALLUM and DAWN MITCHELL

Cataloguing-In-Publication-Data
A CIP catalogue for this book is available from the British Library.

ISBN: 0600 59282 0

Printed and bound in China

Contents

Introduction 6

BIRTHS 8
Moses Basket 10
Bear Repeat 11
Animal Sampler 12
Stork and Baby 14
Toy Sampler 16

BIRTHDAYS 18
Little Girl's 1st Birthday 20
Little Boy's 1st Birthday 21
Girl's 18th Birthday (Key) 22
Girl's 18th or 21st (Wild Rose) 23
Boy's 18th or 21st (Motorbike) 24
Boy's 18th or 21st (Key) 26
Man's 70th/80th/90th Birthday 27
Woman's 70th/80th/90th Birthday 28

ENGAGEMENTS AND WEDDINGS 30
Engagement Congratulations 32
Wedding Congratulations 33
Wedding Congratulations and Place Card 34
Wedding Sampler 36
Silver Anniversary 38

GOOD LUCK 40
Good Luck 42
New Job 43
New Home 44
Exams 46
Travel or Moving Abroad 47
Driving Test 48
Visit to Hospital 50
Get Well Soon 51

SPECIAL OCCASIONS 52
Happy New Year 54
New Year Chimney Sweep 55
Valentine's Day 56
Easter Chick 57
Easter Cross 58
Mother's Day 59
Father's Day 60

CHRISTMAS 62
Santa 64
Poinsettia 66
Holly and Ivy 67
Robin 68
Winter Scene 70
Fireplace and Stockings 71
Children's Toys 72

FLORAL GREETINGS 74
Roses 76
Forget-me-nots 78
Honeysuckle 79
Arum Lilies 80
Poppies 82
Bluebells 83
Daisies 84
Tulips 86
Sunflowers 87

DESIGN SOURCES 88
Motifs 90
Borders 94
Alphabets 98
Numbers 102

MATERIALS AND TECHNIQUES 104
Basic Equipment 106
The Stitches 108
Getting Ready to Stitch 109
Mounting the Cards 110

Suppliers 111
Index and Acknowledgements 112

Introduction

Cross stitch and greeting cards are a combination which work well. So often stitchers accumulate boxes of work with lovingly stitched pictures, neatly stored and not touched for years. It's the stitching that's important and once it's in a stitcher's head to sew, nothing will stop them from doing so. However, if they're stitching for a purpose – for a celebration or a special occasion – the time spent sewing is so much more enjoyable, and a hand-stitched greeting card is always given from the heart. Much as they enjoy the stitching alone, a finished design, beautifully mounted and delivered to someone special, is one of the most satisfying moments for any cross stitcher.

Once mastered, cross stitch is an effective medium for creating superb pictures. It is often compared to painting by numbers, something I'm sure we've all turned our hand to at some time or other, usually with

pretty dismal results. But only a stitcher can turn a colour chart into a work of art on canvas. Forget about the paintbrush –

with cross stitch everyone can become an artist, interpreting colours and symbols in their own way, and making every picture a personal triumph.

In **Cross Stitch Greeting Cards** you can choose from more than 50 original designs, all specially picked to celebrate the touching times of life. Some of Britain's best cross stitch designers have contributed to this collection. It spans from birth to retirement, covering all the precious moments in-between. And, if you're feeling inspired, turn to the motif library at the end of the book to add personal touches to your design.

I started sewing when I was eight. I can remember being handed some binca, thread and a piece of graph paper and being told to make it into a table mat. The teacher showed us the basic stitch and then left us to it. I have an extremely clear memory of designing and stitching a rooster into a corner of the fabric and then fraying the edges of the mat. It was great fun. I gave it to my mum as a present, she loved it, and the mat sat on top of the TV for the best part of the next ten years. As a child I had no inhibitions about stitching - I was shown how to do it and so I did. And as I've grown older I've approached every new craft with the same enthusiasm and lack of inhibition. It doesn't matter if you make mistakes, so long

as you have a go. You'll find you learn something from every mistake, until you feel confident enough to say you're an expert, and that's a lovely feeling. Talking to adults who have just started to cross stitch I've discovered that they've lost that childish lack of inhibition, and they often hinder themselves by thinking they're not able to learn something new. I'll tell you now, anyone can cross stitch and it's an addictive hobby that once started can easily turn into a way of life. You may start designing for books or magazines, start having your own kits made, or simply find all your spare time taken up with a needle in your hand.

Julia, my co-author, is a prime example of someone who started out with little confidence in her designs and stitching, yet as time moved on her confidence grew. She started experimenting and designing original work, rather than following other people's designs. With each new design she learnt something about how colours worked, which stitches to use where and how best to mount the finished work, up until now, when I would consider her to be one of the most talented designers I've worked with. Look out for her designs in this book, especially the dainty Easter Cross card and the subtly delicate Honeysuckle. This is the third book on which we have collaborated, and with every design I see she gets better.

In fact, each of the designers who've worked on this book have a distinctive style which you'll probably begin to recognize as you look through. And each has contributed something different from the other, which, hopefully, will mean that there's at least one design here for everyone, from quirky and comical to bold and colourful.

Use the designs as a starting point, and begin to make cards which you'll be proud to send. You'll find all instructions for making the cards on page 108, and instructions for mounting the cards on page 110. Then, as you gain confidence, use the motifs, borders, alphabets and numbers at the back of the book to add your own touch to your designs. For example, you could stitch the motorbike, give it a border and personalize it with a name, then instead of putting it in a card you could have it framed and give it as a present to be hung in a prime position in any home. Remember, you're creating heirlooms that'll be kept for ever. Your cross stitch pictures are your signature, something by which you'll be remembered, and the sentiments you send will be the things that trigger your recipient's memory. The more of yourself you put into a design, the more valued it will be by the recipient.

With greetings for all occasions, you should never find yourself short of ideas for every conceivable celebration. So start stitching!

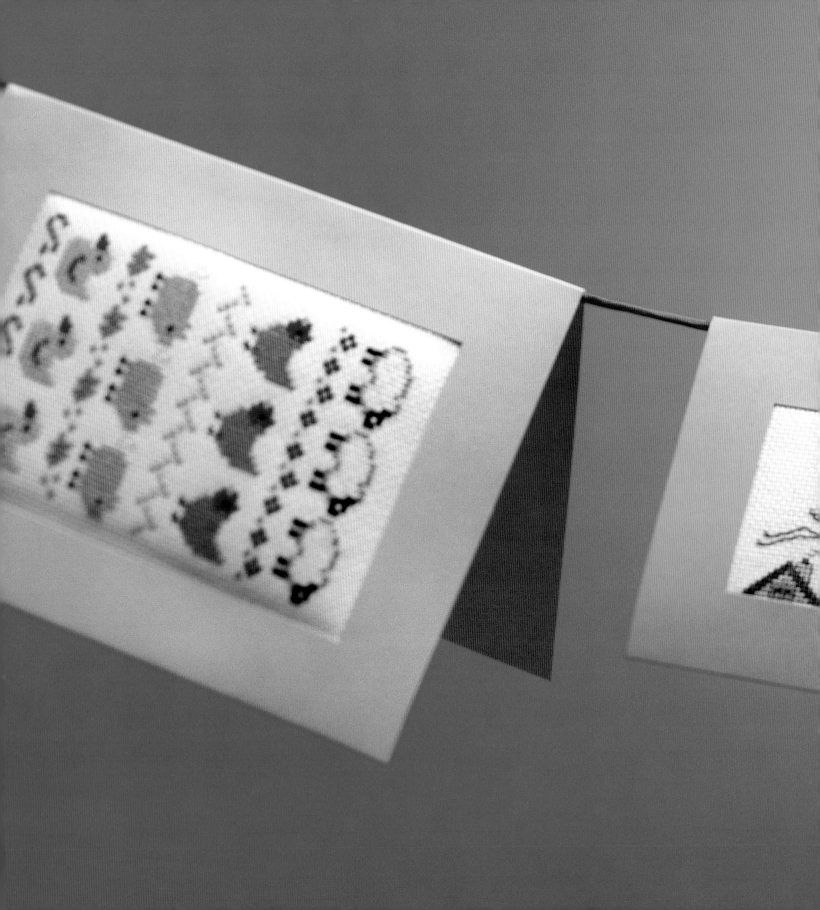

BIRTHS

If you've a friend or someone in the family who's expecting a baby,
mark the occasion with one of these original designs and let them know
how thrilled you are!

Moses Basket

Tucked away in the branches of a blossom tree, a new-born baby gets its first view of the world and everything that awaits him or her. It's an exciting event to capture in thread.

Measurements
The actual cross stitch design measures 10.5 x 6.8cm (4⅛ x 2¾in)

Materials
- 14.5 x 20cm (5¾x 8in) of antique white 27-count evenweave fabric
- One skein of stranded cotton in each colour listed in the key
- Size 26 tapestry needle
- Green card with rectangular opening measuring 11 x 7.5cm (4¼ x 3in)

Note
Evenweave tends to fray more than Aida. Stop this happening by sealing the edge with nail varnish before you start stitching.

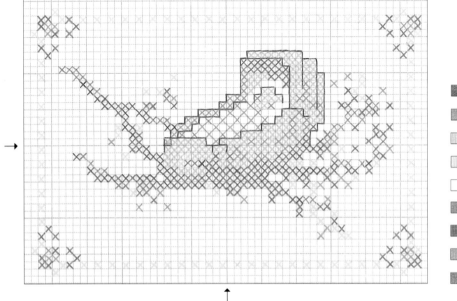

DMC	Anchor		DMC	Anchor
840	379		367	216
729	890		368	214
676	891		3829	901
3774	778			
blanc	1		Back stitch	
3325	129		DMC	Anchor
899	40		840	379
776	24			
841	378			

Bear Repeat

Be there one, two, three or more babies at the same time, this cute teddy bear design can be adapted to suit.

Measurements
The actual cross stitch design measures 11.4 x 5.8cm (4½ x 2¼in)

Materials
- 13 x 15cm (5⅛ x 5⅞in) of white 18-count Aida fabric
- One skein of stranded cotton in each colour listed in the key
- Size 26 tapestry needle
- Pale green card with rectangular opening measuring 11.4 x 7cm (4½ x 2¾in)

Note
Choose the appropriate number and combination of girl or boy bears to suit the set of twins or triplets you are stitching for.

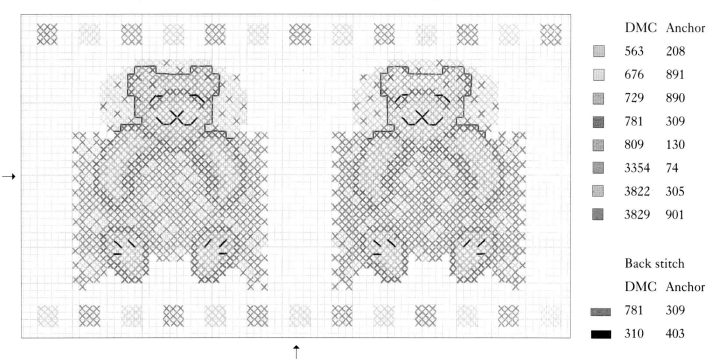

	DMC	Anchor
	563	208
	676	891
	729	890
	781	309
	809	130
	3354	74
	3822	305
	3829	901

Back stitch
	DMC	Anchor
	781	309
	310	403

Animal Sampler

If counting sheep appeals to you, why not try counting pigs, chickens and ducks, too?
This card would look fabulous framed and hung in a nursery.

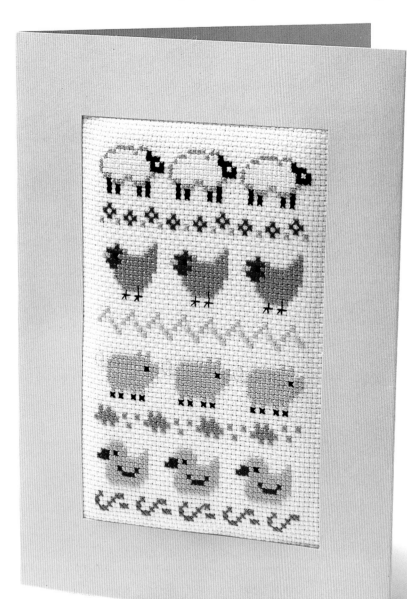

Measurements

The actual cross stitch design measures
8.3 x 13.3cm (3¼ x 5¼in)

Materials

- 14.5 x 20cm (5¾ x 8in) of white 14-count Aida fabric
- One skein of stranded cotton in each colour listed in the key
- Size 26 tapestry needle
- Pink card with rectangular opening measuring 9.5 x 14.5cm (3¾ x 5¾in)

Note

Individual animal motifs taken from this chart could be used to make gift tags or small items such as fridge magnets or keyrings.

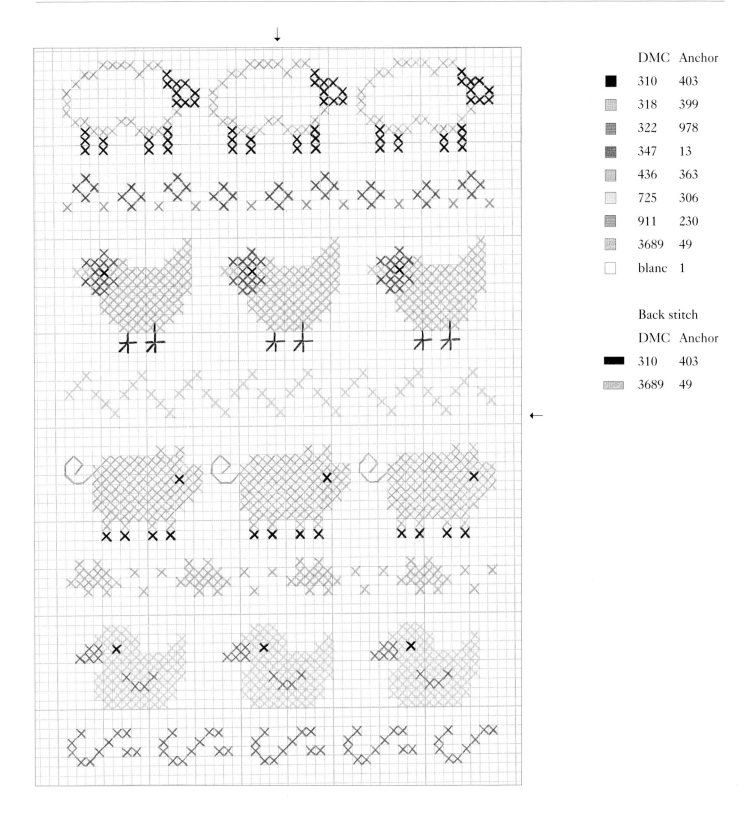

DMC   Anchor

- 310   403
- 318   399
- 322   978
- 347   13
- 436   363
- 725   306
- 911   230
- 3689   49
- blanc   1

Back stitch

DMC   Anchor

- 310   403
- 3689   49

Stork and Baby

Why not make this whimsical card for the proud parents-to-be to mark the imminent arrival of their new-born baby? Add a matching tag to decorate a gift.

Measurements

Card: The actual cross stitch design measures 6.5 x 4.6cm (2⅝ x 1¾in)

Tag: The actual cross stitch design measures 2.5 x 2.6cm (1 x 1in)

Materials

- 13cm (5in) square of white 18-count Aida fabric for card
- 7.6cm (3in) square of white 18-count Aida fabric for tag
- One skein of stranded cotton in each colour listed in the keys
- Size 26 tapestry needle
- Pale blue (or pink) card with rectangular opening measuring 7.6 x 5.7 cm (3 x 2¼in)
- Blue (or pink) gift tag with square opening measuring 4 x 4cm (1½ x 1½in)

Note

If you want to personalize this design, you could make the baby's wrap a different colour and change all the blue to green, pink or yellow.

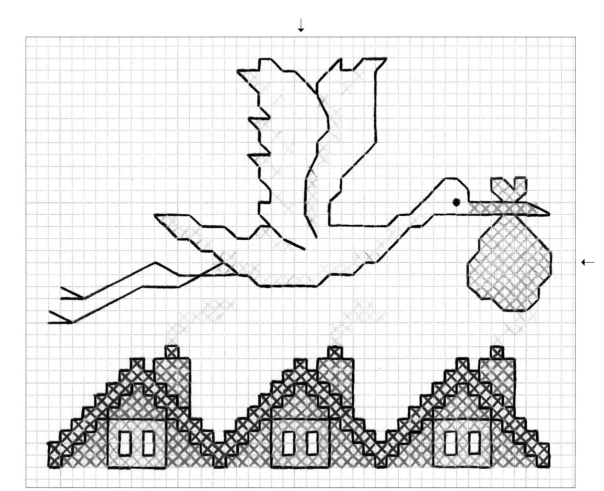

Card

DMC	Anchor
301	349
3072	397
972	298
597	168
3761	928
738	367
blanc	2

Back stitch

DMC	Anchor
3799	236

French knots

DMC	Anchor
3799	236

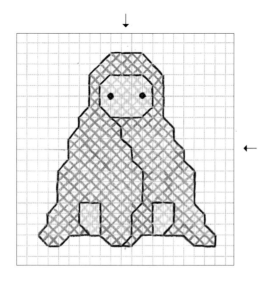

Tag for a boy

DMC	Anchor
819	271
597	168
3761	928

Back stitch

DMC	Anchor
3799	236

French knots

DMC	Anchor
3799	236

Tag for a girl

DMC	Anchor
819	271
962	75

Back stitch

DMC	Anchor
3799	236

French knots

DMC	Anchor
3799	236

Toy Sampler

Why not make a card that's as much a gift as it is a greeting? You could frame this nursery design and it would provide a welcome and permanent reminder of childhood.

Measurements
The actual cross stitch design measures 12.2 x 8.5cm (4⅝ x 3⅜in)

Materials
- 14.5 x 20cm (5¾ x 8in) of white 14-count Aida fabric
- One skein of stranded cotton in each colour listed in the key

- Size 26 tapestry needle
- Red card with rectangular opening measuring 15 x 10cm (6 x 4in)

Note
Use the numbers and alphabets from the back of the book to personalize this card, with a name and date of birth.

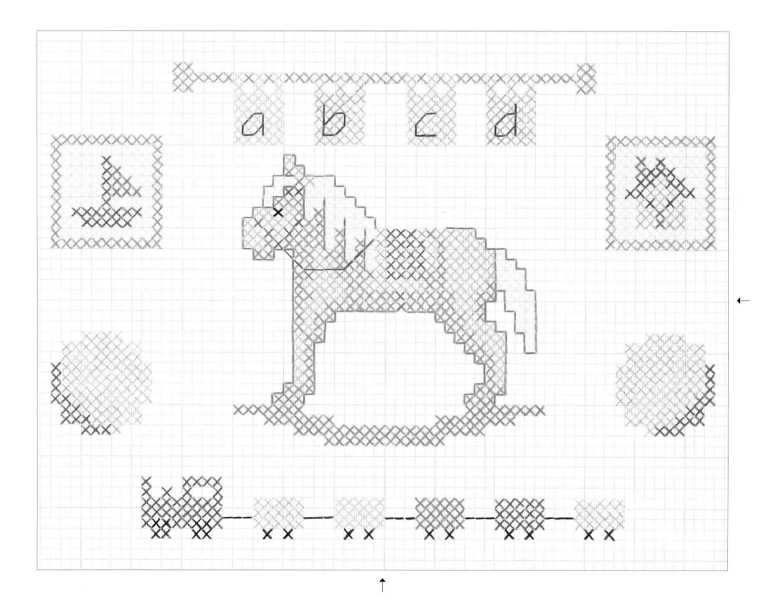

DMC	Anchor		DMC	Anchor		Back stitch		
						DMC	Anchor	
310	403		563	208		347	13	alphabet
322	978		677	300		322	978	horse's reins
347	13		726	295		435	901	horse's body and mane
435	901		809	130		310	403	train
436	363		3689	49				
562	210							

BIRTHDAYS

There's nothing more special than a thoughtfully stitched greeting for a friend or loved one. A hand-made card is also a gift that'll be kept and treasured for ever.

Little Girl's 1st Birthday

Mark the occasion of this first, special birthday with a party, a present and a hand-stitched card to harness and savour the memory.

Measurements
The actual cross stitch design measures 7.3 x 6.8cm (2⅞ x 2¾in)

Materials
• 13cm (5in) square of white 18-count Aida fabric
• One skein of stranded cotton in each colour listed in the key
• Size 26 tapestry needle
• Pink card with square opening measuring 8.8 x 8.8cm (3½ x 3½in)

	DMC	Anchor
	666	46
	601	77
	604	55
	353	6
	996	433
	975	370
	976	309
	310	403
	blanc	1

Back stitch

	DMC	Anchor
	310	403

French knots

	DMC	Anchor
••	310	403

Little Boy's 1st Birthday

Remember the first birthday, the first cake and the first candle to be blown out? Capture a magic moment which can never be revisited.

Measurements

The actual cross stitch design measures 6.5 x 6.8cm (2⅝ x 2¾in)

Materials

• 13cm (5in) square of white 18-count Aida fabric
• One skein of stranded cotton in each colour listed in the key
• Size 26 tapestry needle
• Blue card with square opening measuring 8.8 x 8.8cm (3½ x 3½in)

Note

Use the large numbers from the back of this book to make this card suitable for any age of child.

	DMC	Anchor
	797	132
	996	433
	823	150
	353	6
	702	226
	666	46
	743	305
	975	370
	310	403

Back stitch

	DMC	Anchor
	310	403

French knots

	DMC	Anchor
• •	310	403

Girl's 18th Birthday

A pretty, feminine arrangement of ribbons, flowers and the key to the door makes a memorable card for that special 18th birthday.

Measurements

The actual cross stitch design measures 7.2 x 5cm (2⅞ x 2in)

Materials

- 13cm (5in) square of white 14-count Aida fabric
- One skein of stranded cotton in each colour listed in the key
- Size 26 tapestry needle
- Lilac card with rectangular opening measuring 8 x 5.7cm (3⅛ x 2¼in)

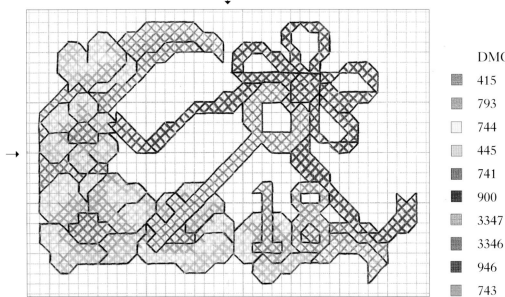

DMC	Anchor
415	398
793	176
744	301
445	288
741	314
900	326
3347	266
3346	267
946	332
743	305

Back stitch

DMC	Anchor
310	403

Girl's 18th or 21st

The wild rose is a beautiful flower and an extremely popular subject for cross stitch. It makes a lovely card for an 18th or 21st birthday.

Measurements

The actual cross stitch design measures 4.5 x 6.8cm (1¾ x 2⅜in)

Materials

• 13cm (5in) square of white 14-count Aida fabric
• One skein of stranded cotton in each colour listed in the key
• Size 26 tapestry needle
• Red card with oval opening measuring 5 x 7.5cm (2 x 3in)

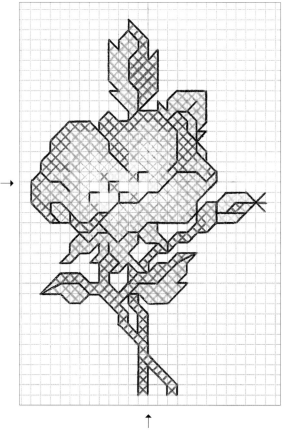

	DMC	Anchor		DMC	Anchor
	700	228		712	926
	701	227		445	288
	699	229		762	234
	913	204			
	335	41		**Back stitch**	
	3326	36		DMC	Anchor
	818	48		310	403
	819	271			

Boy's 18th or 21st

At an age to play, to break the ties and zoom off into the fast lane, this design makes an ideal card. Choose it to mark an eighteenth or twenty-first birthday celebration.

Measurements
The actual cross stitch design measures 13.6 x 8cm (5⅜ x 3⅛in)

Materials
• 14.5 x 20cm (5¾ x 8in) of cream 28-count evenweave fabric
• One skein of stranded cotton in each colour listed in the key
• Size 26 tapestry needle

• Red card with rectangular opening measuring 14.5 x 9.5cm (5¾ x 3¾in)

Note
Omit the number and key from this card to make an ideal greeting for any motorbike enthusiast. A line shows the edge of white cross stitch behind the seat. Do not work as back stitch.

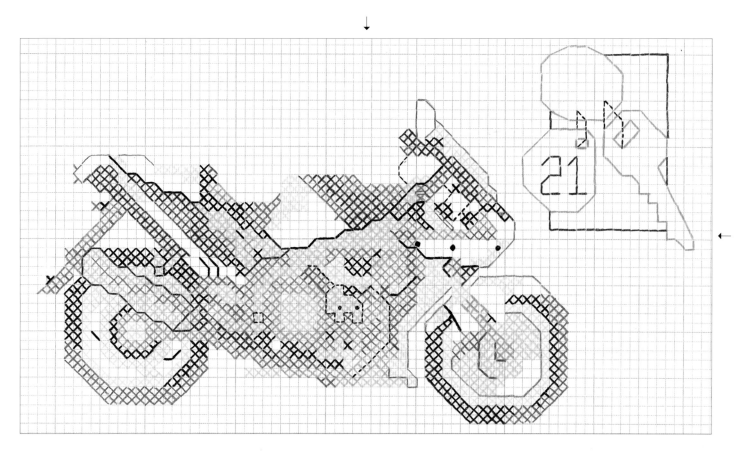

DMC	Anchor		DMC	Anchor
310	403		928	847
350	11		3072	274
413	401		blanc	1
422	943			
543	933			
646	8581		**French knots**	
648	900		DMC	Anchor
666	46		310	403
712	926			
721	324			
840	379			
842	376			
844	273			

Back stitch

1 strand

DMC	Anchor	
310	403	key chain, engine
646	8581	front mudguard, fairing

Back stitch

2 strands

DMC	Anchor	
310	403	under seat and petrol tank
648	900	key and key fob
666	46	numerals and box around key
840	379	main exhaust pipes
blanc	1	handlebars

Boy's 18th or 21st

Think of a favourite pastime and create a card which is unique to the person who'll receive it. In this case, the football fan will be happy.

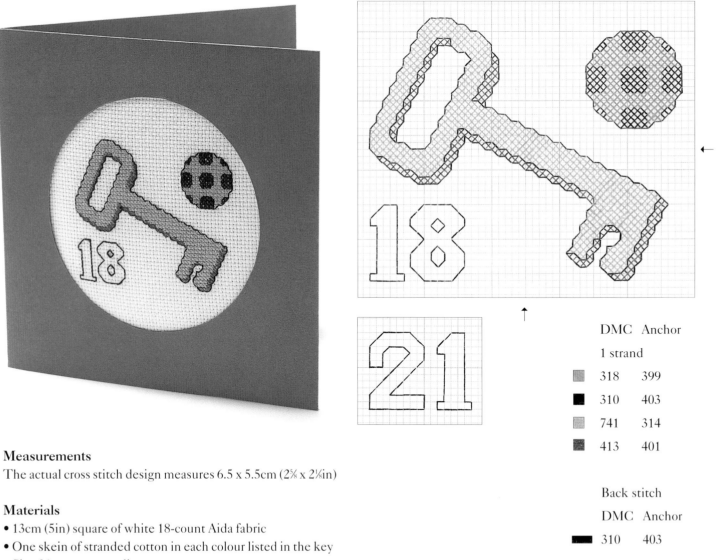

DMC	Anchor
1 strand	
318	399
310	403
741	314
413	401

Back stitch

DMC	Anchor
310	403

Measurements

The actual cross stitch design measures 6.5 x 5.5cm (2⅝ x 2⅛in)

Materials

• 13cm (5in) square of white 18-count Aida fabric

• One skein of stranded cotton in each colour listed in the key

• Size 26 tapestry needle

• Blue card with 8.3cm (3¼in) diameter circular opening

Man's 70th/80th/90th Birthday

At the time of life when all one wants to do is relax and reminisce, this card will trigger memories of all the recipient's favourite hobbies.

Measurements

The actual cross stitch design measures 7.2 x 6.2cm (2⅞ x 2½in)

Materials

- 13cm (5in) square of white 18-count Aida fabric
- One skein of stranded cotton in each colour listed in the key
- Size 26 tapestry needle
- Bright green card with square opening measuring 8 x 8cm (3⅛ x 3⅛in)

Note

If, after stitching, you find your work has become a little dirty, wash it in lukewarm water in a mild solution of washing-up liquid. Leave it to soak, then rinse. Do not wring it out, just dry on a flat surface.

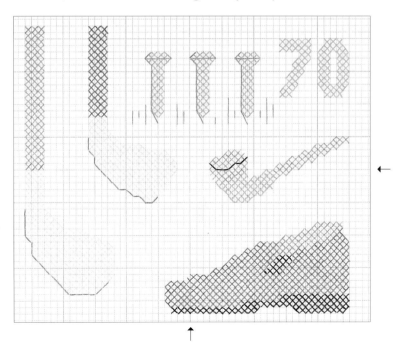

DMC	Anchor		Back stitch		
1 strand			DMC	Anchor	
954	225		310	403	pipe
781	309		924	849	golf tees and
301	349				club heads
738	361		954	225	grass
3072	847				
927	849				
310	403				

Woman's 70th/80th/90th Birthday

The impact of dainty violets pouring out from the top of this flower-filled basket make this a spectacular card. Choose it as a card to send on a friend or relative's retirement.

Measurements

The actual cross stitch design measures 10.8 x 8.5cm (4¼ x 3⅜in)

Materials

• 20 x 14.5cm (8 x 5¾in) of white 28-count evenweave fabric
• One skein of stranded cotton in each colour listed in the key

• Size 26 tapestry needle
• Purple card with rectangular opening measuring 14.5 x 9.5cm (5¾ x 3¾in)

Note

Always stitch over two threads when working on evenweave, to give the same final measurements as over one block of Aida.

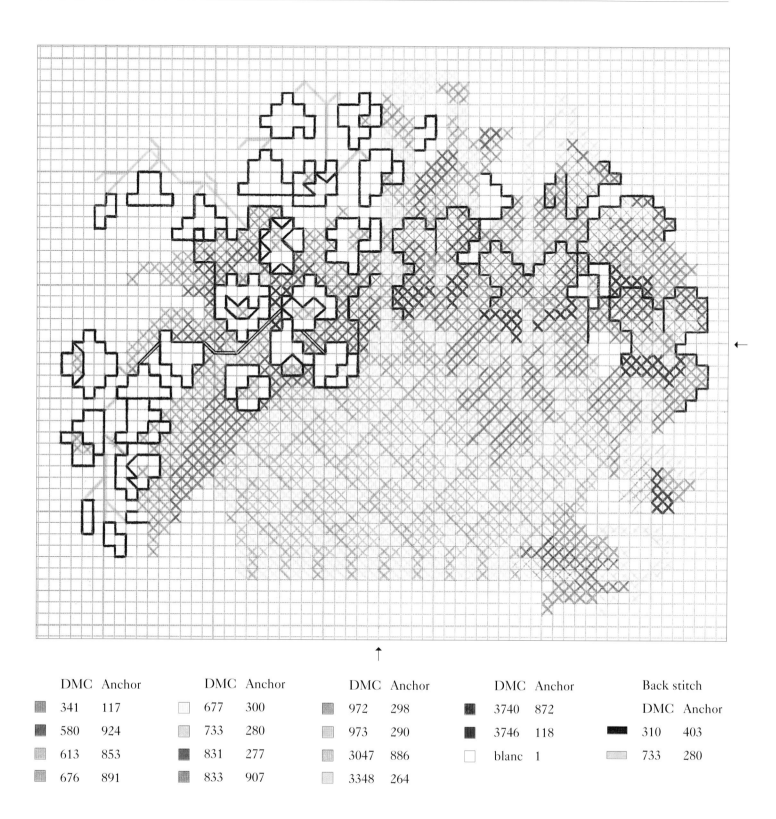

	DMC	Anchor		DMC	Anchor		DMC	Anchor		DMC	Anchor	Back stitch		
	341	117		677	300		972	298		3740	872		DMC	Anchor
	580	924		733	280		973	290		3746	118		310	403
	613	853		831	277		3047	886		blanc	1		733	280
	676	891		833	907		3348	264						

ENGAGEMENTS AND WEDDINGS

Who's getting married in the morning? Whoever it is, you won't be the one to miss the celebration. Join in the merriment and sew!

Engagement Congratulations

It could be the happiest day of your life, and it's certainly one which will be remembered for ever. Take the tipple and stitch this design to commemorate the day.

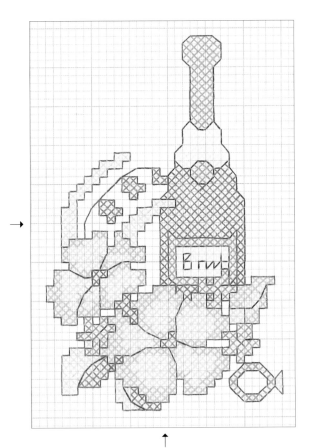

Measurements
The actual cross stitch
design measures 4.5 x 6.8cm (1¾ x 2¾in)

Materials
• 13cm (5in) square of white 18-count Aida fabric
• One skein of stranded cotton in each colour listed in the key
• Size 26 tapestry needle
• Yellow card with rectangular opening measuring 5.7 x 7.5cm (2¼ x 3in)

Note
You could make this card equally suitable for a wedding by omitting to stitch the diamond on the ring.

	DMC	Anchor		DMC	Anchor
	973	290		502	877
	783	306		746	386
	445	288			
	210	108		Back stitch	
	776	24		DMC	Anchor
	368	214		801	358

Wedding Congratulations

Tying the knot is a big step and probably one of the biggest things to change your life. Let the happy couple know how pleased you are for them on their big day.

Measurements
The actual cross stitch design measures 4.8 x 6.5cm (1⅞ x 2⅝in)

Materials
- 13cm (5in) square of white 18-count Aida fabric
- One skein of stranded cotton in each colour listed in the key
- Size 26 tapestry needle
- White card with rectangular opening measuring 5.7 x 7.5cm (2¼ x 3in)

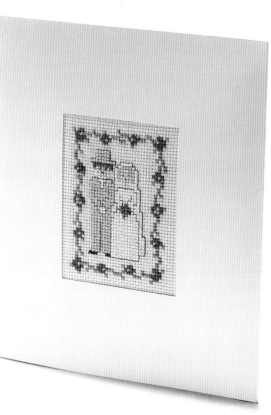

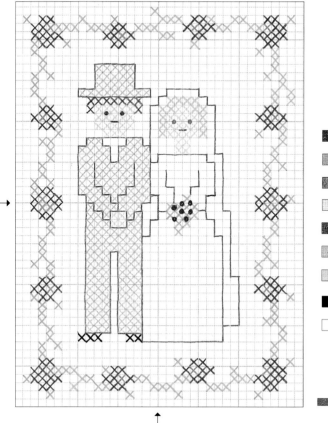

DMC	Anchor
309	39
3341	328
701	227
951	1011
433	371
4150	398
726	297
310	403
blanc	2

Back stitch

DMC	Anchor
317	400

French knots

DMC	Anchor	
309	39	mouths and bouquet
433	371	groom's eyes
798	131	bride's eyes

Wedding Congratulations and Place Card

This elegant wedding greeting makes a perfect gift for the happy couple and is guaranteed to be treasured. Add place cards for the top table, or even every guest if you're very ambitious.

Measurements

Card: The actual cross stitch design measures 8 x 13.2cm (3⅛ x 5¼in)

Place card: The actual cross stitch design measures 5.3 x 3.8cm (2⅛ x 1½in)

Materials
- 14.5 x 20cm (5¾ x 8in) of white 14-count Aida fabric for card
- 7.5 x 10cm (3 x 4in) of white 18-count Aida fabric for place card
- One skein of stranded cotton in each colour listed in the key
- Size 26 tapestry needle
- Salmon pink card with rectangular opening measuring 9 x 14cm (3½ x 5½in)
- Salmon pink gift tag with rectangular opening measuring 6.2 x 4.6cm (2½ x 1¾in)

Note

To make the place card, choose a corner of the main design and stitch it on to a small piece of fabric which can then be mounted into the tag. Cross stitch the place card with one strand of thread.

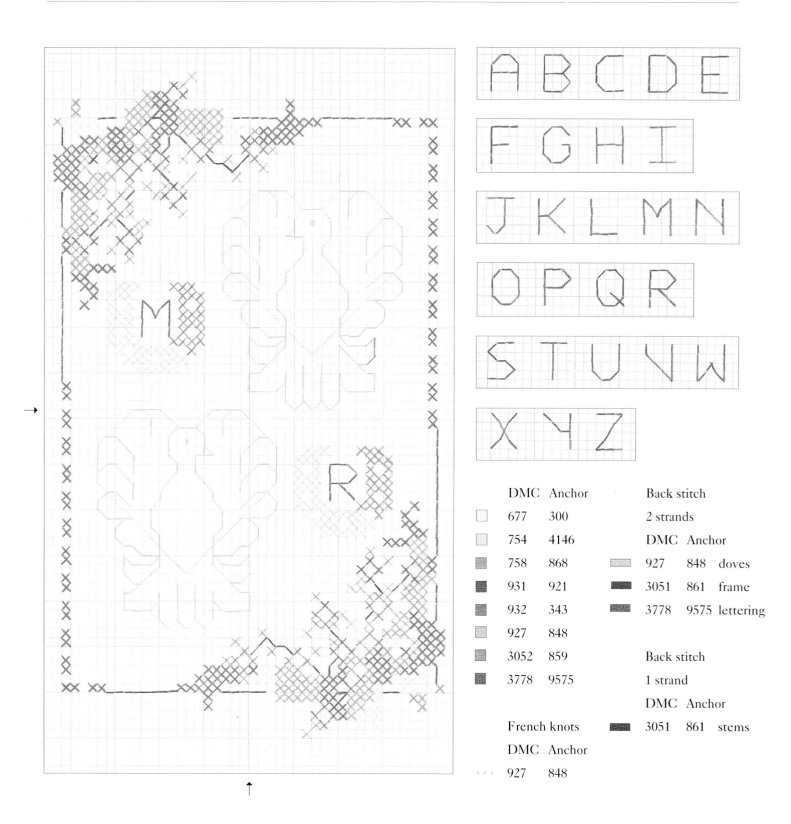

DMC   Anchor   Back stitch
                    2 strands
☐ 677   300
▨ 754   4146   DMC   Anchor
▨ 758   868   ▤ 927   848   doves
▨ 931   921   ▦ 3051 861   frame
▨ 932   343   ▨ 3778 9575   lettering
▨ 927   848
▨ 3052   859   Back stitch
▨ 3778   9575   1 strand
                    DMC   Anchor
French knots   ▬ 3051 861   stems
DMC   Anchor
· · · 927   848

Wedding Sampler

These peaceful doves and gold rings intertwined as a symbol of nascent love make a touching sentiment for a perfect match.

Measurements

The actual cross stitch design measures
9 x 14.3cm (3½ x 5⅝in)

Materials

- 14.5 x 20cm (5¾ x 8in) of antique white
  27-count evenweave fabric
- One skein of stranded cotton in each colour
  listed in the key
- Size 26 tapestry needle
- White card with rectangular opening
  measuring 10.5 x 15.7cm (4⅛ x 6⅛in)

Note

Why not add the initials of the bride and groom to
this card for a truly personal gift? You'll find a
selection of letters beginning on page 98.

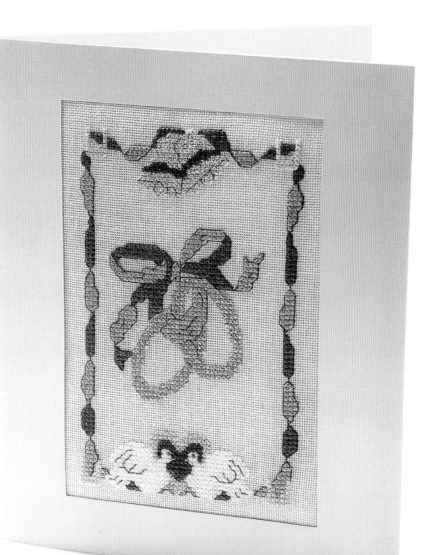

DMC   Anchor

☐ blanc 1

■ 3350   78

■ 3687   68

▨ 776   25

▨ 762   234

▨ 1 strand DMC 725
   (Anchor 305) with
   1 strand gold thread

▨ 1 strand DMC 762
   (Anchor 234) with
   1 strand silver thread

Back stitch
DMC   Anchor

▨ 3350   78   ribbon

▨ 762   234 doves' outlines

▨ 317   400 wings, bells, rings

French knots
DMC Anchor

••• 317   400

Silver Anniversary

Let the bells ring out to 25 years of wedded bliss! Now that's something which should be celebrated. Stitch these sparkling silver bells for a special congratulatory greeting.

Measurements
The actual cross stitch design measures
7.5 x 12.4cm (3 x 4⅞in)

Materials
- 14.5 x 20cm (5¾ x 8in) of antique white
  27-count evenweave fabric
- One skein of stranded cotton in each colour
  listed in the key
- Size 26 tapestry needle
- Lavender card with oval opening measuring
  9.5 x 14.5cm (3¾ x 5¾in)

Note
If you'd like to personalize this card, use one of the alphabets from the back of the book. Use transparent grid paper to trace the letters from the chart and then transfer them on to the design.

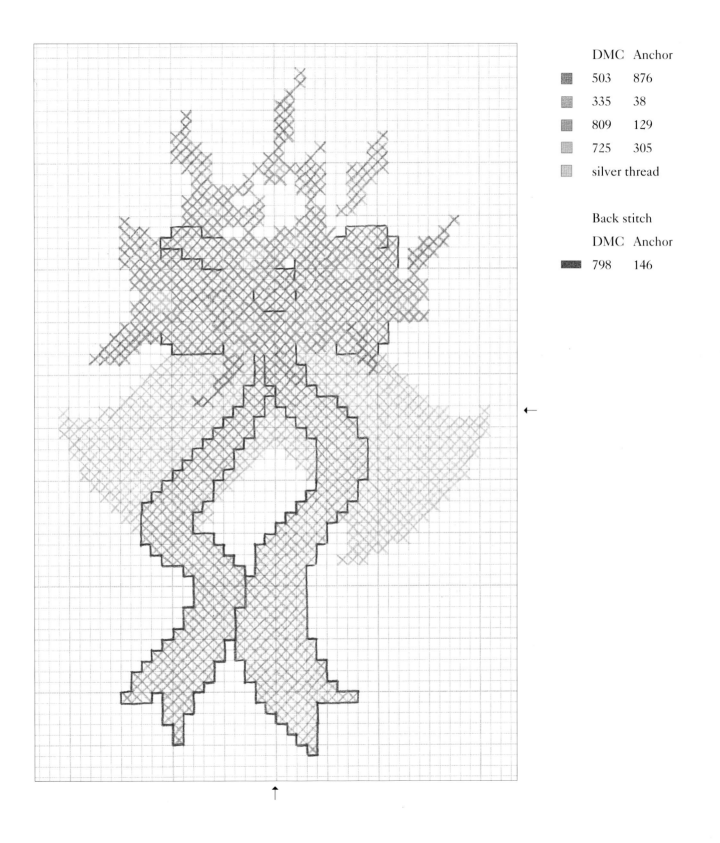

DMC   Anchor

503   876

335   38

809   129

725   305

silver thread

Back stitch

DMC   Anchor

798   146

GOOD LUCK

There's a great sense of achievement every time you accomplish something that could change your life. Here are a selection of cards to commemorate those moments, and one or two that simply wish 'good luck!'.

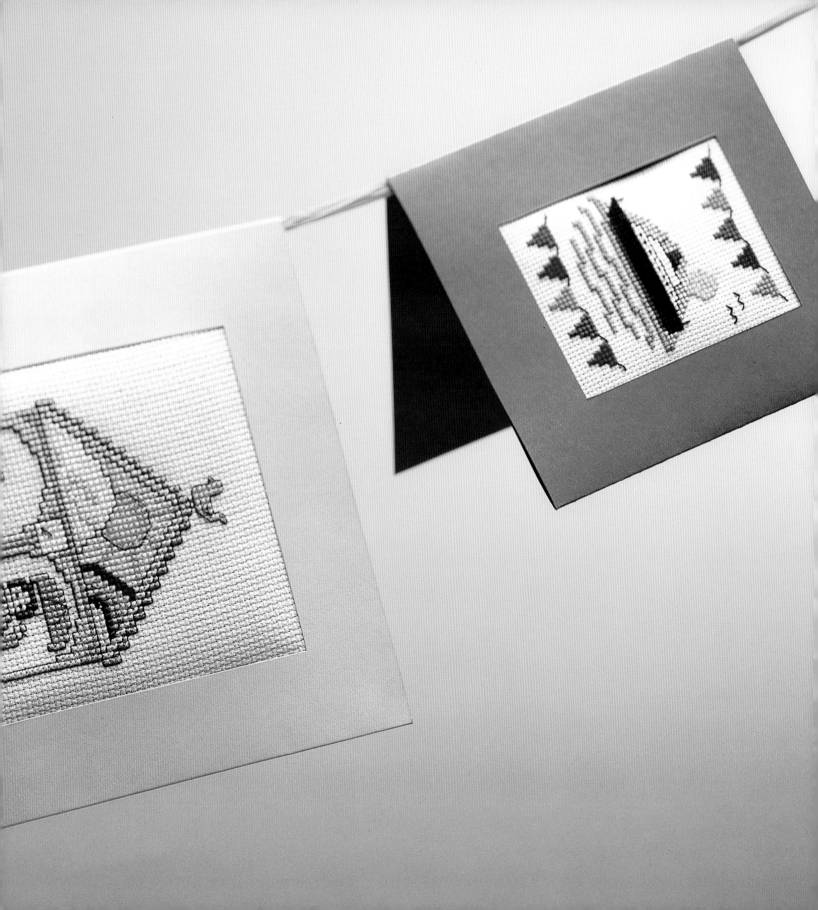

Good Luck

We all deserve a little good luck. Let someone know you wish them well and send them this optimistic and quick to stitch greeting.

Measurements

The actual cross stitch design measures 5 x 7.2cm (2 x 2⅞in)

Materials

- 13 x 15cm (5 x 6in) of white 18-count Aida fabric
- One skein of stranded cotton in each colour listed in the key
- Size 26 tapestry needle
- Dark blue card with oval opening measuring 6.8 x 10cm (2¾ x 4in)

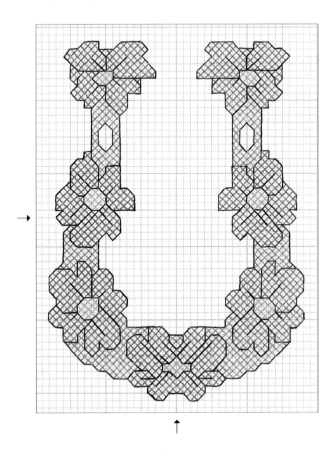

	DMC	Anchor
	834	874
	793	122
	524	858

Back stitch

	DMC	Anchor
	310	403

New Job

Changing your job is a stressful experience, yet we all know how a change can be as good as a rest. Mark the changes with this congratulatory card.

Measurements
The actual cross stitch design measures 7.3 x 5cm (2⅞ x 2in)

Materials
- 13cm (5in) square of white 18-count Aida fabric
- One skein of stranded cotton in each colour listed in the key
- Size 26 tapestry needle
- Bright green card with rectangular opening measuring 7.6 x 5.7cm (3 x 2¼in)

Note
This card would be equally appropriate to celebrate a promotion at work.

	DMC	Anchor
	414	235
	453	231
	3078	292
	975	370
	3828	373
	444	291
	740	316
	353	6
	666	46
	310	403
	blanc	1
	519	167

	DMC	Anchor
	958	187
	704	238

Back stitch

	DMC	Anchor	
	740	316	dress
	975	370	legs, mouth, hands
	958	187	flower stems
	414	235	wall chart

French knots

	DMC	Anchor
•••	975	370

New Home

Moving house is one of the biggest, most expensive and considered decisions ever. It's certainly not an event that should go unnoticed.

Measurements
The actual cross stitch design measures
7.6 x 12.4cm (3⅛ x 4¾in)

Materials
- 14.5 x 20cm (5¾ x 8in) of white 14-count Aida fabric
- One skein of stranded cotton in each colour listed in the key
- Size 26 tapestry needle
- Light green card with rectangular opening measuring 9.5 x 14.5cm (3¾ x 5¾in)

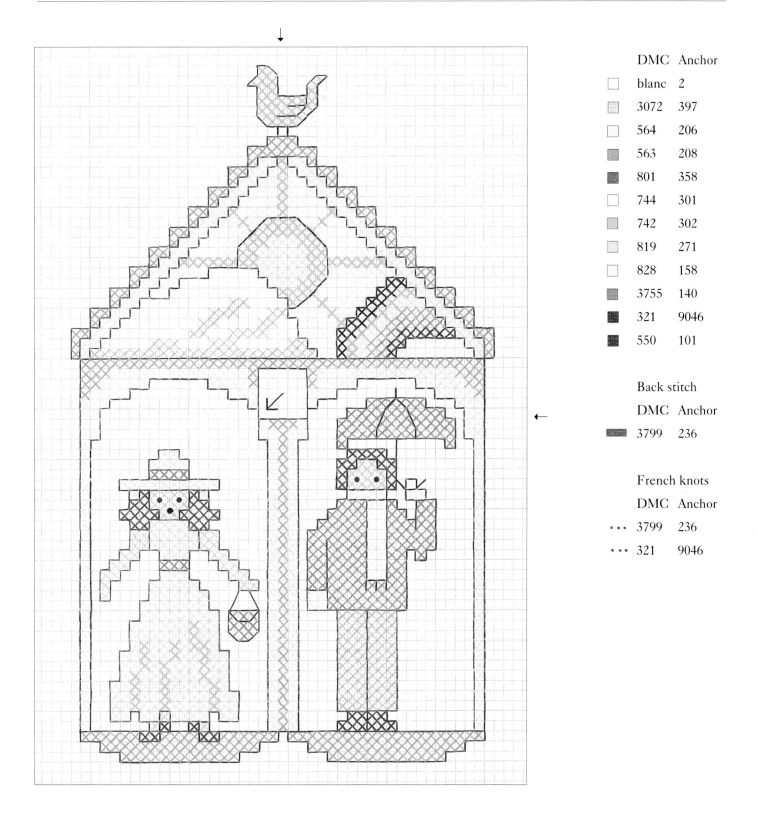

	DMC	Anchor
	blanc	2
	3072	397
	564	206
	563	208
	801	358
	744	301
	742	302
	819	271
	828	158
	3755	140
	321	9046
	550	101

Back stitch

	DMC	Anchor
	3799	236

French knots

	DMC	Anchor
···	3799	236
···	321	9046

Exams

Hats off to the person with the results. A big celebration is in order, whether the recipient has sat a degree, passed school exams or achieved a professional set.

Measurements

The actual cross stitch design measures 5 x 6.5cm (2 x 2⅜in)

Materials

- 13cm (5in) square of white 18-count Aida fabric
- One skein of stranded cotton in each colour listed in the key
- Size 26 tapestry needle
- Dark green card with rectangular opening measuring 5.7 x 7.5cm (2¼ x 3in)

To make a tassel

1 Cut two pieces of thin card approximately 3cm (1⅛in) wide and place together.
2 Wind a length of stranded cotton (all six strands) several times around both cards.
3 Pass a needle containing one strand of cotton between the cards and tie the tassel together at one end. Leave the ends of this thread long.
4 Cut through the tassel at the other end and then remove the cards. Keeping the threads folded in half, wind a single strand around the top of the tassel several times. Pass the end of this strand through the wound thread to cast off.
5 Use the thread from stage 3 to stitch the tassel onto the card as indicated on the chart.

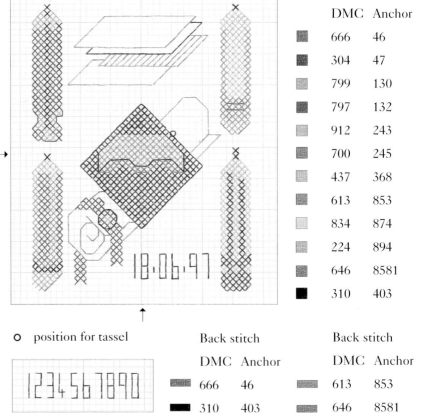

DMC	Anchor
666	46
304	47
799	130
797	132
912	243
700	245
437	368
613	853
834	874
224	894
646	8581
310	403

o   position for tassel

Back stitch			Back stitch	
DMC	Anchor		DMC	Anchor
666	46		613	853
310	403		646	8581

Travel or Moving Abroad

If a friend moves abroad or takes an extended trek into the wide blue yonder, this card will fit the occasion perfectly.

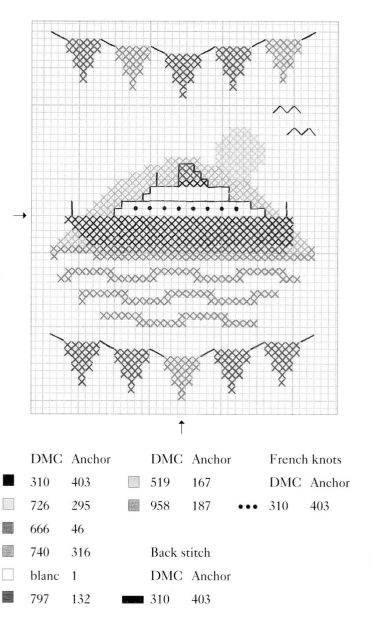

Measurements
The actual cross stitch design measures 5.2 x 7.6cm (2¹⁄₁₆ x 3in)

Materials
- 13cm (5in) square of white 18-count Aida fabric
- One skein of stranded cotton in each colour listed in the key
- Size 26 tapestry needle
- Blue card with rectangular opening measuring 5.7 x 8.3cm (2¼ x 3¼in)

	DMC	Anchor		DMC	Anchor		French knots	
■	310	403		519	167		DMC	Anchor
	726	295		958	187	•••	310	403
	666	46						
	740	316		Back stitch				
	blanc	1		DMC	Anchor			
	797	132	▬	310	403			

Driving Test

You've cause for celebration if you've just passed your driving test. This is definitely a card for a careful driver. Who do you know who deserves one?

Measurements

The actual cross stitch design measures 13.2 x 8cm (5¼ x 3⅛in)

Materials

• 14.5 x 20cm (5¾ x 8in) of white 14-count Aida fabric

• One skein of stranded cotton in each colour listed in the key

• Size 26 tapestry needle

• Dark green card with retangular opening measuring 14.5 x 9.5cm (5¾ x 3¾in)

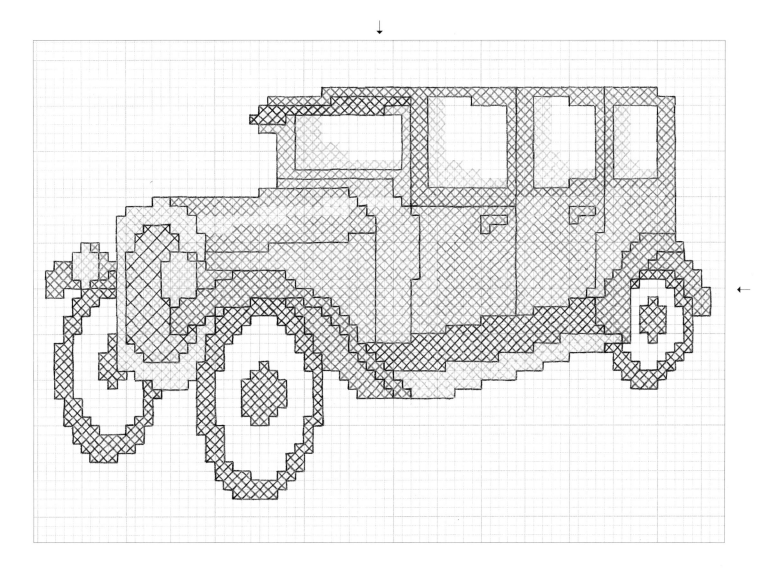

	DMC	Anchor		DMC	Anchor	Back stitch
	3032	832		318	399	
	783	306		524	858	DMC Anchor
	310	403		3362	263	310 403
	blanc	2		3363	262	
	640	393		522	860	

Visit to Hospital

The rabbit's in a sorry state with his bandaged ear and paw, but he's sure to cheer up anybody who's not feeling one hundred per cent.

Measurements

The actual cross stitch design measures 5.5 x 8cm (2⅛ x 3⅛in)

Materials

- 13 x 15cm (5 x 6in) of white 18-count Aida fabric
- One skein of stranded cotton in each colour listed in the key
- Size 26 tapestry needle
- Turquoise card with rectangular opening measuring 6.2 x 8.5cm (2½ x 3⅜in)

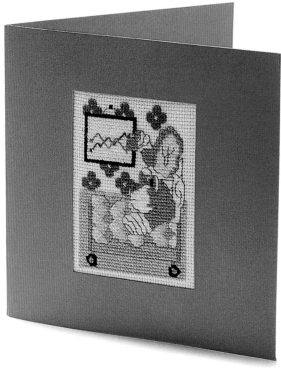

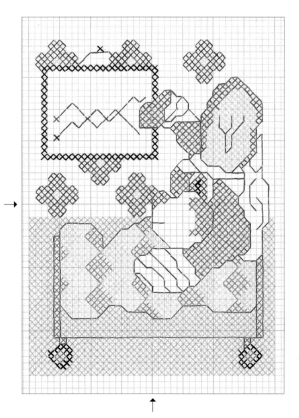

	DMC	Anchor			DMC	Anchor	
☐	blanc	1			955	240	
■	310	403			602	41	
	318	235			552	99	
	762	399					
	798	142			**Back stitch**		
	3325	130			DMC	Anchor	
	307	289			317	400	bed, rabbit, string
	819	271			304	799	red line on wall chart
	420	374			798	142	blue line on wall chart

Get Well Soon

They say flowers are always appreciated and cheering. Why not give flowers to someone you know who's a little under the weather?

Measurements
The actual cross stitch design measures 4.7 x 6.5cm
(1⅞ x 2⅜in)

Materials
- 13cm (5in) square of white 18-count Aida fabric
- One skein of stranded cotton in each colour listed in the key
- Size 26 tapestry needle
- Red card with rectangular opening measuring 7 x 9cm (2¾ x 3½in)

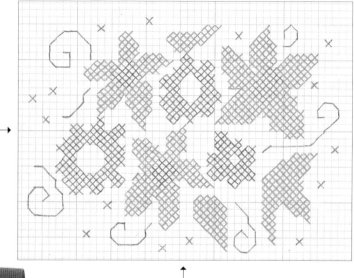

DMC	Anchor		Back stitch	
1 strand			DMC	Anchor
3778	9575		3042	870
3726	970			
977	313			
3042	870			

SPECIAL OCCASIONS

Mark key days in the year with a stitched greeting card to help your family and friends remember those days over the years to come.

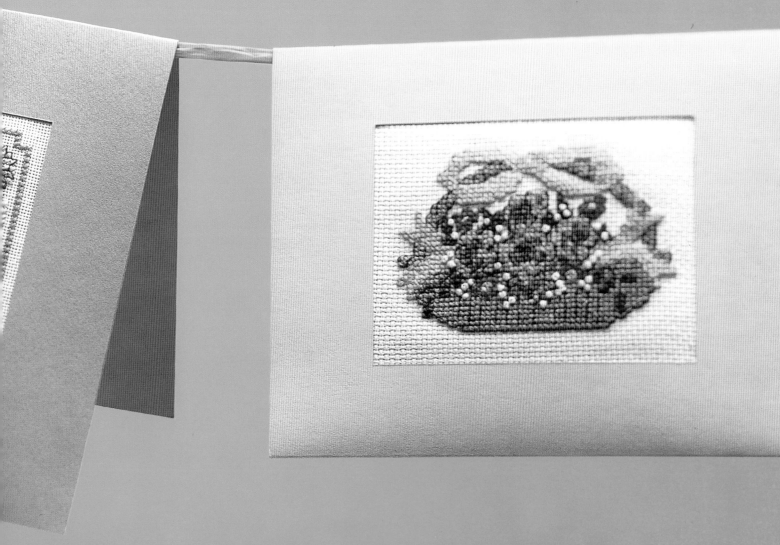

Happy New Year

Let the New Year in with a celebration tipple and look forward to the promising times ahead.

Measurements
The actual cross stitch design measures 5 x 7.3cm (2 x 2⅞in)

Materials
- 13cm (5in) square of white 18-count Aida fabric
- One skein of stranded cotton in each colour listed in the key
- Size 26 tapestry needle
- Blue card with rectangular opening measuring 6 x 8cm (2⅜ x 3⅛in)

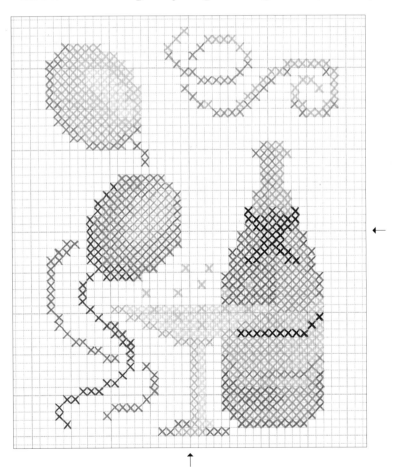

	DMC	Anchor		DMC	Anchor
	209	109		677	300
	310	403		783	307
	327	100		815	22
	553	98		3765	169
	554	97		3812	189
	646	8581		3818	246
	648	900		3820	874
	676	891			

New Year Chimney Sweep

People used to believe a chimney sweep brought luck for the New Year. Welcome a sweep into a friend's home with this cheerful card.

Measurements

The actual cross stitch design measures 5 x 7.5cm (2 x 3in)

Materials

- 13 x 15cm (5 x 6in) of white 18-count Aida fabric
- One skein of stranded cotton in each colour listed in the key
- Size 26 tapestry needle
- Bright red card with rectangular opening measuring 7.5 x 10cm (3 x 4in)

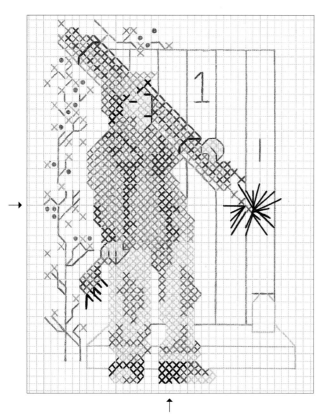

	DMC	Anchor
■	310	403
▨	646	8581
▨	838	380
▨	840	379
▨	841	378
▨	844	273
▨	900	326
▨	951	880
▨	3045	888
▨	3046	887
▨	3346	267
☐	3770	276

Long stitch

	DMC	Anchor
▬	310	403

French knots

	DMC	Anchor
••••	900	326

Back stitch

1 strand

	DMC	Anchor	
▬	310	403	face
▬	840	379	branches
▬	844	273	around face, hands and door knob

Back stitch

2 strands

	DMC	Anchor	
▨	646	8581	step and bottle
▨	838	380	around rods
▨	3045	888	rods
▨	3046	887	rods and bottle top
▨	3346	267	door

Valentine's Day

Keep him guessing with this Victorian-inspired, hand-stitched Valentine Day's card.

Measurements
The actual cross stitch design measures 7.7 x 7.8cm (3¹⁄₁₆ x 3¹⁄₁₆in)

Materials
- 13cm (5in) square of antique white 27-count evenweave fabric
- One skein of stranded cotton in each colour listed in the key
- Size 26 tapestry needle
- Pink card with square opening measuring 8.6 x 8.6cm (3⅜ x 3⅜in)

	DMC	Anchor		Back stitch	
				DMC	Anchor
	963	73			
	677	885		3350	65
	962	75		3051	861
	523	859			

Note
Before you send this card, why not add a couple of drops of scent to add a further air of mystery? No one will ever know who sent it!

Easter Chick

Choose this cute, newly-born chick to make an enchanting Easter card.

Measurements

The actual cross stitch design measures 7.1 x 6cm (2¾ x 2⅜in)

Materials

• 13cm (5in) square of white 18-count Aida fabric

• One skein of stranded cotton in each colour listed in the key

• Size 26 tapestry needle

• Yellow card with 8.3cm (3¼in) diameter circular opening

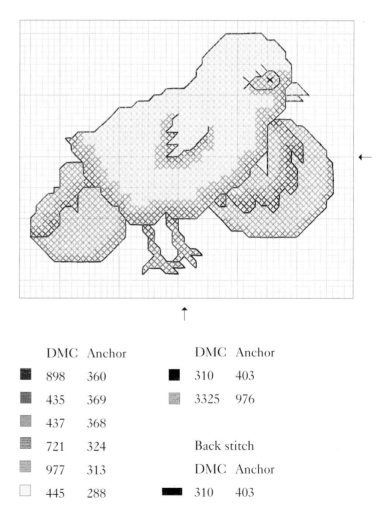

DMC	Anchor		DMC	Anchor
898	360		310	403
435	369		3325	976
437	368			
721	324		**Back stitch**	
977	313		DMC	Anchor
445	288		310	403

Easter Cross

Remember the true meaning of Easter with this attractively dainty, seasonal greeting.

Measurements
The actual cross stitch design measures 4.3 x 6.5cm (1¾ x 2⅝in)

Materials
- 13cm (5in) square of white 18-count Aida fabric
- One skein of stranded cotton in each colour listed in the key
- Size 26 tapestry needle
- Yellow card with rectangular opening measuring 5.7 x 7.5cm (2¼ x 3in)

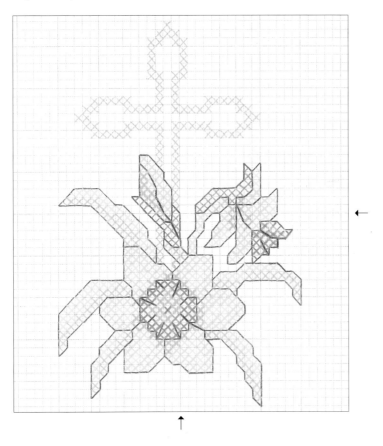

	DMC	Anchor		Back stitch
	3072	397		DMC	Anchor
	445	288		801	358
	973	290			
	437	368			
	972	298			
	742	303			
	772	259			
	471	265			

Mother's Day

Let your mother know how much you care by making her this original card.

Measurements

The actual cross stitch design measures 5.5 x 8cm (2⅛ x 3⅛in)

Materials

- 13 x 15cm (5 x 6in) of white 18-count Aida fabric
- One skein of stranded cotton in each colour listed in the key
- Size 26 tapestry needle
- Yellow card with rectangular opening measuring 6.2 x 8.5cm (2½ x 3⅜in)

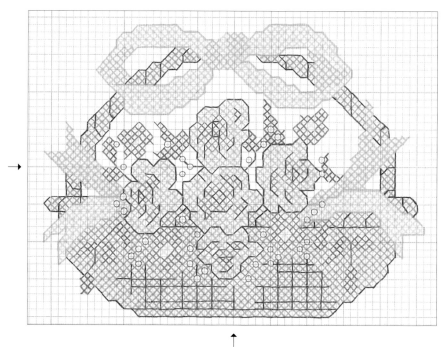

	DMC	Anchor
▨	335	41
▨	3716	25
▨	3345	268
▨	729	890
▨	972	298
▨	726	295
▨	798	131
☐	727	293

French knots

	DMC	Anchor
○○○	746	275

Back stitch
1 strand

	DMC	Anchor	
▬	600	78	roses
▬	780	310	basket
▬	972	298	ribbon and bow

Back stitch
2 strands

	DMC	Anchor	
▬	3345	268	stems and leaves

Father's Day

As the years pass by, picture this tranquil scene, epitomizing the luxury of having time on your hands to do with as you will.

Measurements

The actual cross stitch design measures 8 x 14.3cm (3⅛ x 5⅝in)

Materials

- 14.5 x 20cm (5¾ x 8in) of white 14-count Aida fabric
- One skein of stranded cotton in each colour listed in the key
- Size 26 tapestry needle
- Bright blue card with rectangular opening measuring 9 x 15cm (3½ x 6in)

Note

There are a lot of threads for this card. Keep them handy by making your own thread sorter out of the cardboard from tights or shirt packaging.

To make a thread sorter

1 Use a hole punch to make holes down the side of a piece of thin card. Make as many holes as there are threads used in the design.
2 Number each hole with the appropriate thread number.
3 Loop cut lengths of the threads through the appropriate hole.

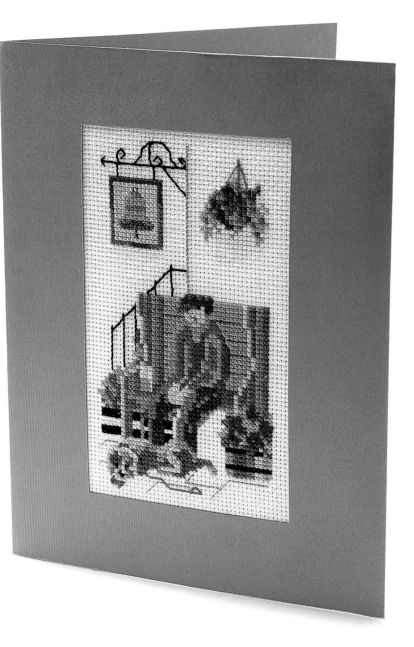

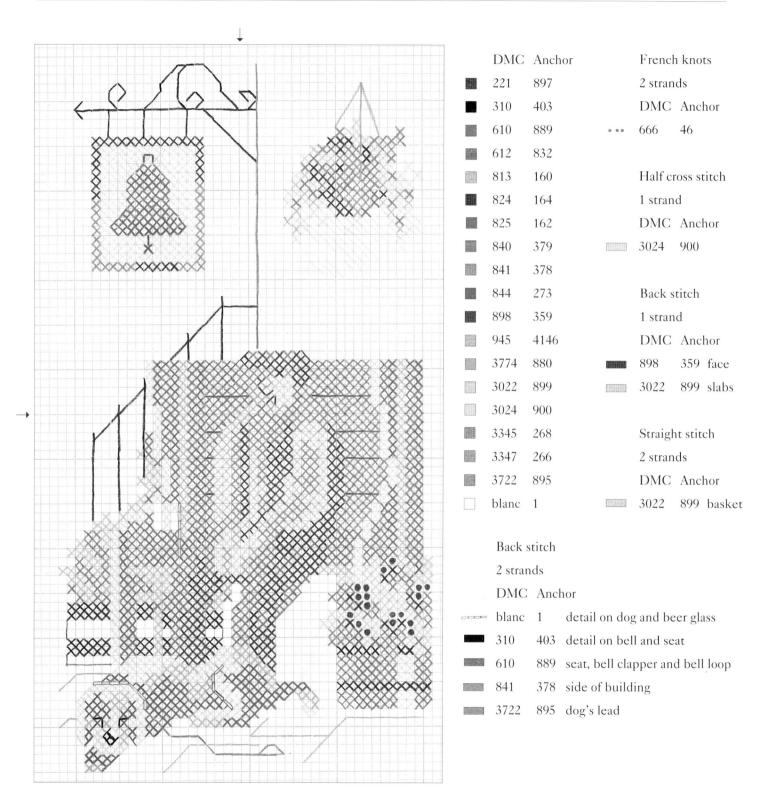

DMC	Anchor		
221	897		
310	403		
610	889		
612	832		
813	160		
824	164		
825	162		
840	379		
841	378		
844	273		
898	359		
945	4146		
3774	880		
3022	899		
3024	900		
3345	268		
3347	266		
3722	895		
blanc	1		

French knots
2 strands

DMC	Anchor	
666	46	

Half cross stitch
1 strand

DMC	Anchor	
3024	900	

Back stitch
1 strand

DMC	Anchor	
898	359	face
3022	899	slabs

Straight stitch
2 strands

DMC	Anchor	
3022	899	basket

Back stitch
2 strands

DMC	Anchor	
blanc	1	detail on dog and beer glass
310	403	detail on bell and seat
610	889	seat, bell clapper and bell loop
841	378	side of building
3722	895	dog's lead

CHRISTMAS

A Christmas cross stitch greeting can be brought out year after year as part of the Yuletide decorations.

Santa

If you're looking for a challenging and substantial project, have a go at stitching Santa.
He'd make a perfect card, or you could frame him instead!

Measurements
The actual cross stitch design measures
13 x 8.2cm (5 x 3¼in)

Materials
- 14.5 x 20cm (5¾ x 8in) of white 14-count Aida fabric
- One skein of stranded cotton in each colour listed in the key
- Size 26 tapestry needle
- Red card with rectangular opening measuring 11 x 15cm (4¼ x 6in)

Note
Although this Santa makes a good card it could equally well be framed and kept as a Christmas keepsake which could be brought out each year. On the chart, note that white cross stitch is outlined to show where it finishes. Do not work this as back stitch.

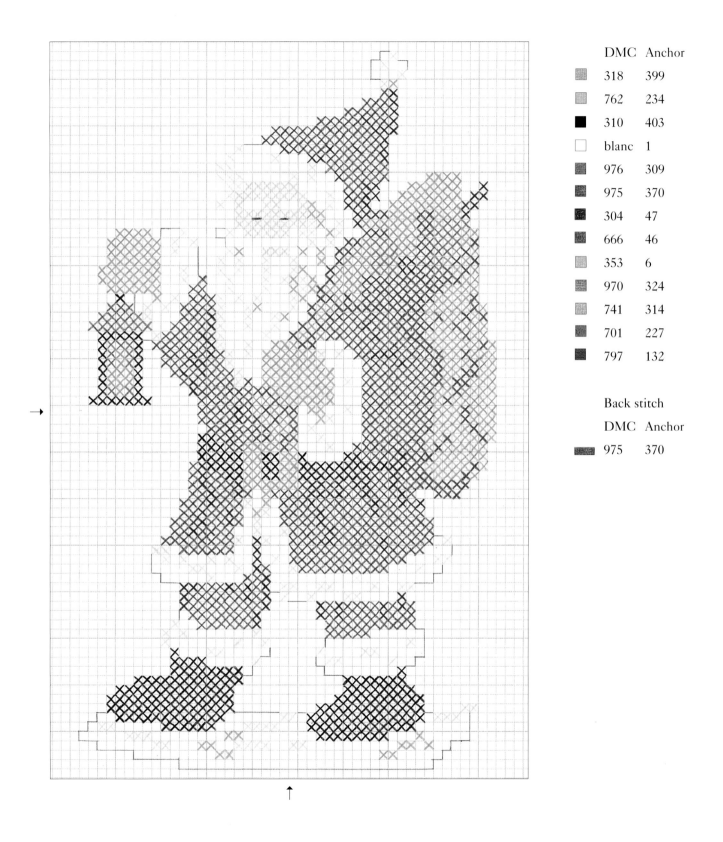

DMC	Anchor
318	399
762	234
310	403
blanc	1
976	309
975	370
304	47
666	46
353	6
970	324
741	314
701	227
797	132

Back stitch

DMC	Anchor
975	370

Poinsettia

The poinsettia epitomizes the spirit of Christmas. With its bright red flowers and deep green leaves you can't go wrong.

Measurements
The actual cross stitch design measures 6.8 x 6.8cm (2¾ x 2¾in)

Materials
- 13cm (5in) square of white 18-count Aida fabric
- One skein of stranded cotton in each colour listed in the key
- Size 26 tapestry needle
- Purple card with 8cm (3⅛in) diameter circular opening

	DMC	Anchor
■	816	1005
▨	347	13
▨	351	10
▨	907	255
☐	3348	253

Back stitch		
	DMC	Anchor
▬	938	381

French knots		
	DMC	Anchor
•••	972	298

Holly and Ivy

Christmas wouldn't be Christmas without a touch of holly and ivy. Deck your mantel with this festive card.

Measurements
The actual cross stitch design measures 5.4 x 6.5cm (2⅛ x 2⅝in)

Materials
- 13cm (5in) square of white 18-count Aida fabric
- One skein of stranded cotton in each colour listed in the key
- Size 26 tapestry needle
- Green card with rectangular opening measuring 6.8 x 8cm (2¾ x 3⅛in)

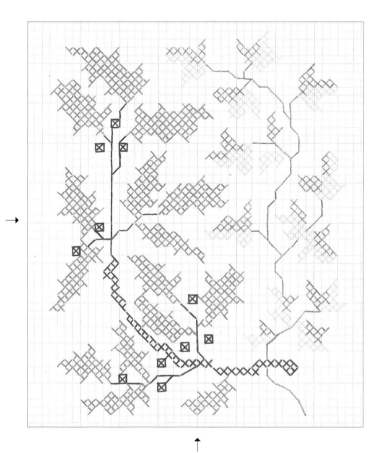

DMC	Anchor		Back stitch		
1 strand			DMC	Anchor	
469	267		469	267	ivy stems
472	278		319	217	holly stems
817	19				
319	217				
699	229				

Note
Why not try using red seed beads for the berries in this card? It is an unusual and very effective touch.

Robin

There's nothing more endearing than seeing a robin looking for scraps in the snow.
Don't you just want to take him home and look after him!

Measurements
The actual cross stitch design measures 12.7 x 7.5cm (4⅞ x 3in)

Materials
• 20 x 14.5cm (8 x 5¾ in) of white 14-count Aida fabric

• One skein of stranded cotton in each colour listed in the key
• Size 26 tapestry needle
• Dark green card with oval opening measuring 14.5 x 9.5cm (5¾ x 3¾ in)

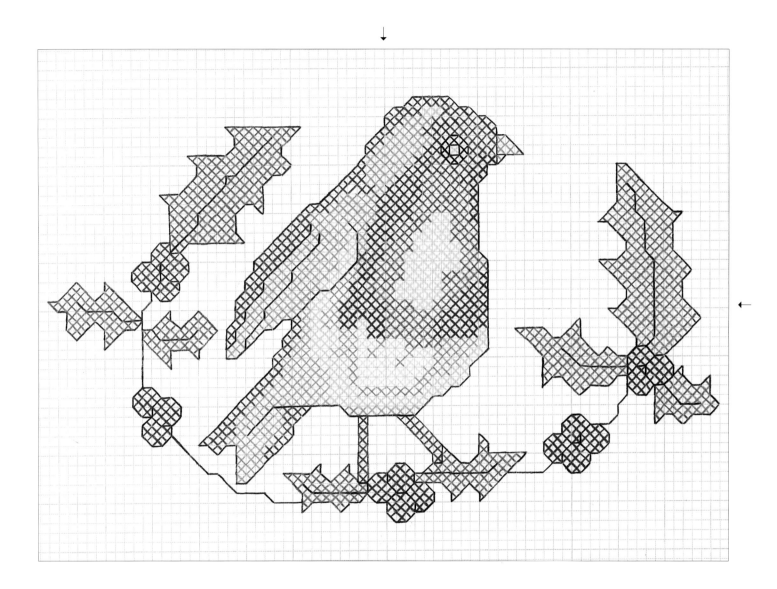

	DMC	Anchor		DMC	Anchor		DMC	Anchor	Back stitch
	3362	263		739	366		225	892	DMC Anchor
	310	403		ecru	387		666	46	310 403
	801	359		415	398				
	435	369		304	47				

Winter Scene

*A snow-covered landscape looks beautiful.
Picture snow-peaked roofs to conjure up an
idyllic image of crisp winter days.*

Measurements
The actual cross stitch design measures 5.5 x 6.8cm (2⅛ x 2⅜in)

Materials
• 13cm (5in) square of white 18-count Aida fabric
• One skein of stranded cotton in each colour listed in the key
• Kreinik blending filament
• Size 26 tapestry needle
• Lavender card with rectangular opening measuring 6.8 x 8cm (2¾ x 3⅛in)

	DMC	Anchor				
			Half cross stitch			
	3689	73	1 strand			
	3350	77	DMC	Anchor		
	210	109	3354	74		
	208	111	3350	77		
	794	120	794	120		
	797	132	797	132		
	742	303				
	300	357	**Back stitch**			
	613	853	DMC	Anchor		
	3011	856	300	357	church cross	
	503	876	Kreinik metallic			
	699	923	sky blue (014)	lower line, icicle and		
	501	878		snow details		

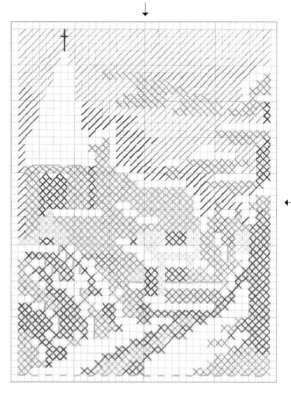

Fireplace and Stockings

...and while you're waiting for Santa to come and fill your stocking, you could cuddle up in front of a warm, glowing, cheery fire.

Measurements

The actual cross stitch design measures 4.6 x 6.6cm (1¾ x 2⅝in)

Materials

- 13cm (5in) square of white 18-count Aida fabric
- One skein of stranded cotton in each colour listed in the key
- Size 26 tapestry needle
- Red card with rectangular opening measuring 5.7 x 7.5cm (2¼in x 3in)

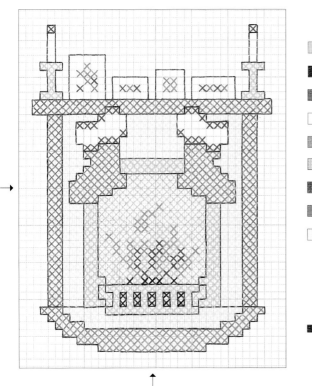

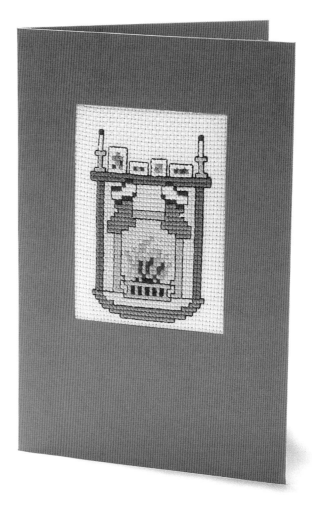

DMC	Anchor
972	298
310	403
975	370
blanc	2
741	314
3072	397
321	9046
701	227
746	386

Back stitch

DMC	Anchor
310	403

Note

Small ends of Kreinik thread worked into the flames of the fire will give them life and add a crackle and sparkle to this design.

Children's Toys

Remember when you were young? How pleased would you have been to receive a card like this? Or better still the toys themselves!

Measurements

The actual cross stitch design measures 12.5 x 8.3cm (4¾ x 3¼in)

Materials

- 14.5 x 20cm (5¾ x 8in) of white 14-count Aida fabric
- One skein of stranded cotton in each colour listed in the key
- Size 26 tapestry needle

- Yellow card with rectangular opening measuring 14.3 x 10.5cm (5⅝ x 4⅛in)

Note

If you've untold patience and want a truly awesome project, why not repeat this design to make a stunning fabric shelf border for a child's room? For a larger project still, you could use it as the mainstay of a room design.

	DMC	Anchor		DMC	Anchor	Back stitch
■	310	403	▨	776	24	1 strand
□	blanc	1	▨	677	300	DMC Anchor
▨	726	297	▨	3607	87	▬ 317 400 waistcoat outline, bricks, doll, soldier, balloon and
▨	225	892	▨	334	977	bow tie
▨	224	894	▨	471	265	▬ 433 357 bear's outline, bear's cheeks and tummy button
▨	445	288	▨	413	401	
▨	321	9046				Back stitch
▨	3072	397				2 strands
▨	402	347		French knots		DMC Anchor
▨	701	245		DMC	Anchor	▬ 310 403 bear's muzzle, numbers
▨	797	132	•••	317	400	▬ 321 9046 waistcoat detail

FLORAL GREETINGS

You can't go wrong if you choose to send flowers. They're great for all occasions and for everyone. So, for a foolproof greeting, stitch a bloom.

Roses

If you're an ambitious stitcher this card will provide an ideal challenge. Beautiful big blooms will be a delight to stitch and a joy to receive.

Measurements
The actual cross stitch design measures
21 x 12.5cm (8¼ x 5in)

Materials
• 32 x 25cm (12 x 10in) of antique white
   27-count evenweave fabric
• One skein of stranded cotton in each colour
   listed in the key
• Size 26 tapestry needle
• Burgundy card with oval opening measuring
   22 x 15cm (8⅝ x 5⅞in)

Note
When working a large design like this one, you might find it easier to keep your place on your chart by using a sticky note which you can move around as you complete each bit.

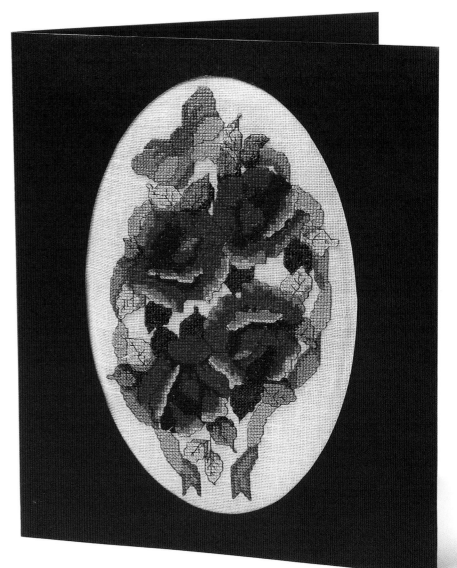

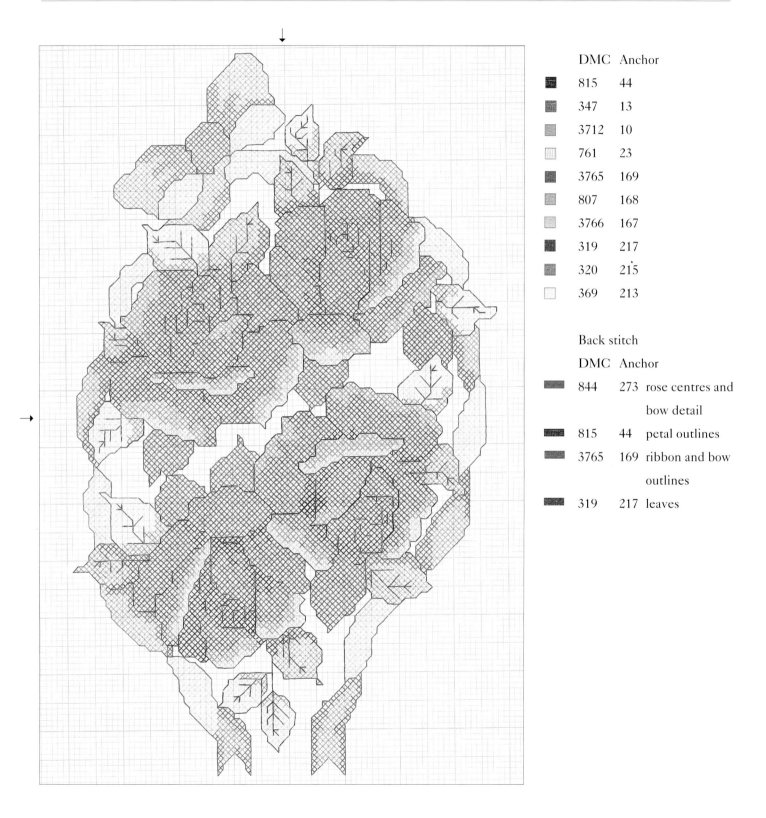

DMC   Anchor

815   44

347   13

3712   10

761   23

3765   169

807   168

3766   167

319   217

320   215

369   213

Back stitch

DMC   Anchor

844   273   rose centres and
                bow detail

815   44   petal outlines

3765 169   ribbon and bow
                outlines

319   217   leaves

Forget-me-nots

Designs don't need to be complicated to be good. This simple design could be stitched and sent in an hour. How's that for made to order?

Measurements
The actual cross stitch design measures
6.8 x 4.8cm (2¾ x 1⅞in)

Materials
- 13cm (5in) square of white 14-count Aida fabric
- One skein of stranded cotton in each colour listed in the key
- Size 26 tapestry needle
- Lilac card with oval opening measuring 7.5 x 5.5cm (3 x 2⅛in)

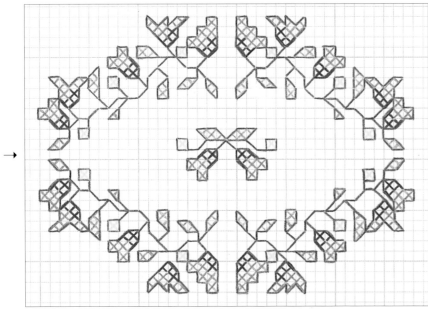

	DMC	Anchor	Back stitch		
				DMC	Anchor
	307	289		890	683
	367	216			
	793	176			
	792	177			

Note
Omit the central floral motif and stitch your own special greeting on this card using letters from one of the alphabets which begin on page 98.

Honeysuckle

This design is so life-like you can almost smell the sweet scent of the delicate flowers.

Measurements

The actual cross stitch design measures 7 x 7.5cm (2¾ x 3in)

Materials

- 13cm (5in) square of white 18-count Aida fabric
- One skein of stranded cotton in each colour listed in the key
- Size 26 tapestry needle
- Yellow card with oval opening measuring 8 x 8.5cm (3⅛ x 3⅜in)

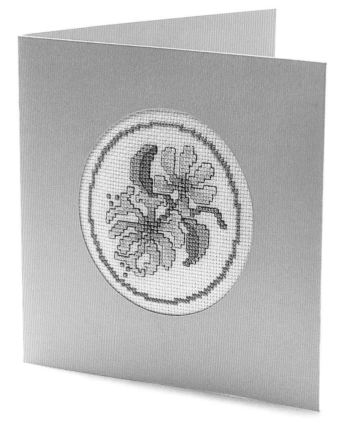

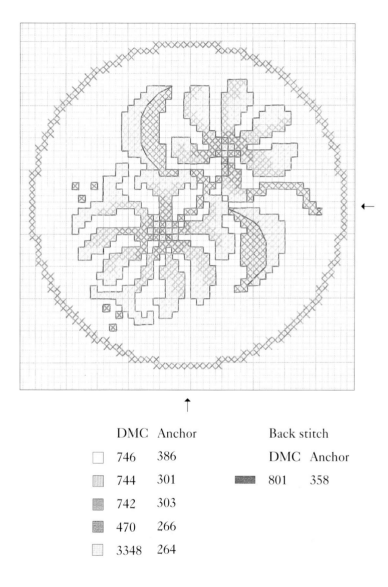

DMC	Anchor		Back stitch	
			DMC	Anchor
746	386			
744	301		801	358
742	303			
470	266			
3348	264			

Note

If you have to unpick your work for any reason and find yourself with bits of fluff, roll them off by wrapping sticky tape around a cotton bud and dabbing it around the fluffy bits of thread.

Arum Lilies

Tall, lean, elegant and pure, that's a common perception of the lily. What a lovely perception to have of someone special. Let them know by sending them this card.

Measurements

The actual cross stitch design measures 9 x 12.8cm (3½ x 5in)

Materials

- 14.5 x 20cm (5¾ x 8in) of white 14-count Aida fabric
- One skein of stranded cotton in each colour listed in the key
- Size 26 tapestry needle
- Cream card with rectangular opening measuring 10.5 x 14cm (4⅛ x 5½in)

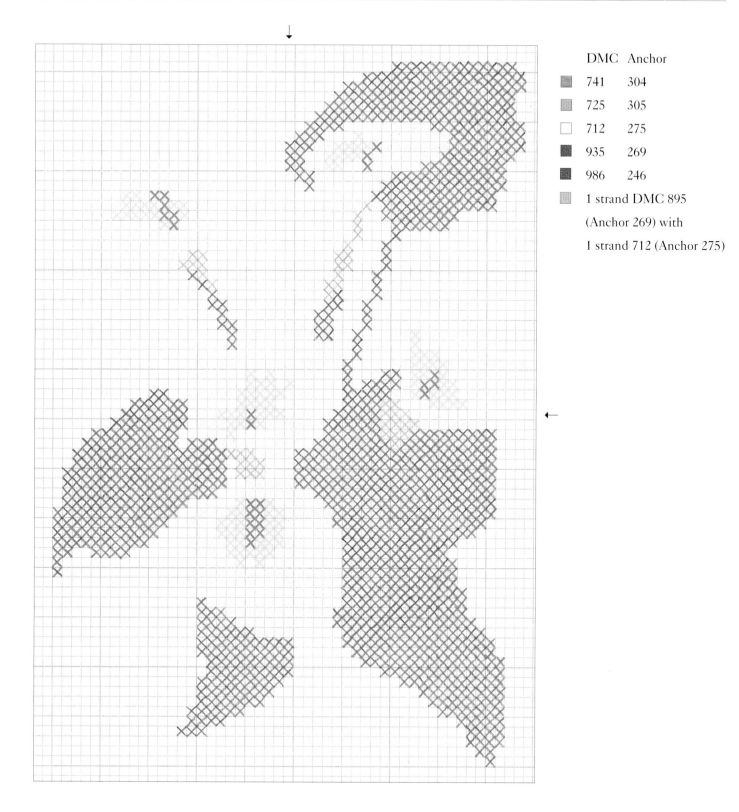

DMC   Anchor
741   304
725   305
712   275
935   269
986   246
1 strand DMC 895
(Anchor 269) with
1 strand 712 (Anchor 275)

Poppies

Cheerful poppies make a striking greeting ideal for livening up someone's special day.
This easy-to-stitch design can be worked by even the most novice stitcher.

Measurements
The actual cross stitch design measures 3.6 x 7cm
(1⅜ x 2¾in)

Materials
• 13cm (5in) square of white 14-count Aida fabric

• One skein of stranded cotton in each colour
  listed in the key
• Size 26 tapestry needle
• Mauve card with oval opening measuring
  5 x 7.5cm (2 x 3in)

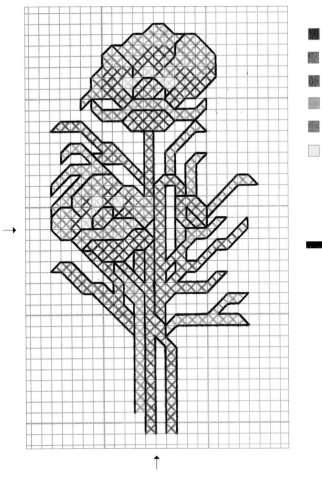

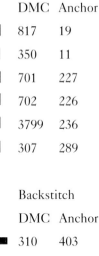

DMC	Anchor
817	19
350	11
701	227
702	226
3799	236
307	289

Backstitch

DMC	Anchor
310	403

Bluebells

The bluebell is one of spring's most beautiful gems. When you see its rich blue flower you know it's a harbinger of the coming summer.

Measurements

The actual cross stitch design measures 4.8 x 7.5cm (1⅞ x 3in)

Materials

- 13cm (5in) square of white 18-count Aida fabric
- One skein of stranded cotton in each colour listed in the key
- Size 26 tapestry needle
- Bright green card with rectangular opening measuring 6 x 8cm (2⅜ x 3⅛in)

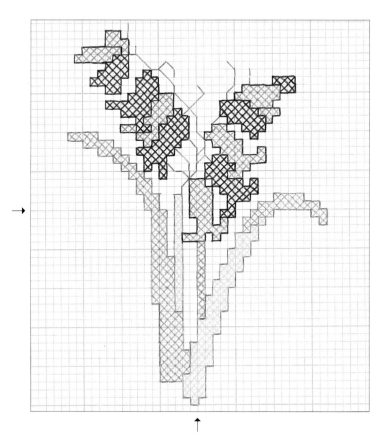

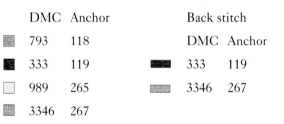

	DMC	Anchor		Back stitch	
				DMC	Anchor
	793	118		333	119
	333	119		3346	267
	989	265			
	3346	267			

Daisies

Daisies may be simple flowers, but if you want to send a special message their simplicity makes them the perfect choice! Stitch them into a pretty chain.

Measurements

The actual cross stitch design measures 7.5 x 11cm (3 x 4⅜in)

Materials

- 14.5 x 20cm (5¾ x 8in) of cream 18-count Aida fabric
- One skein of stranded cotton in each colour listed in the key
- Size 26 tapestry needle
- Lilac card with oval opening measuring 9.5 x 13.5cm (3¾ x 5⅜in)

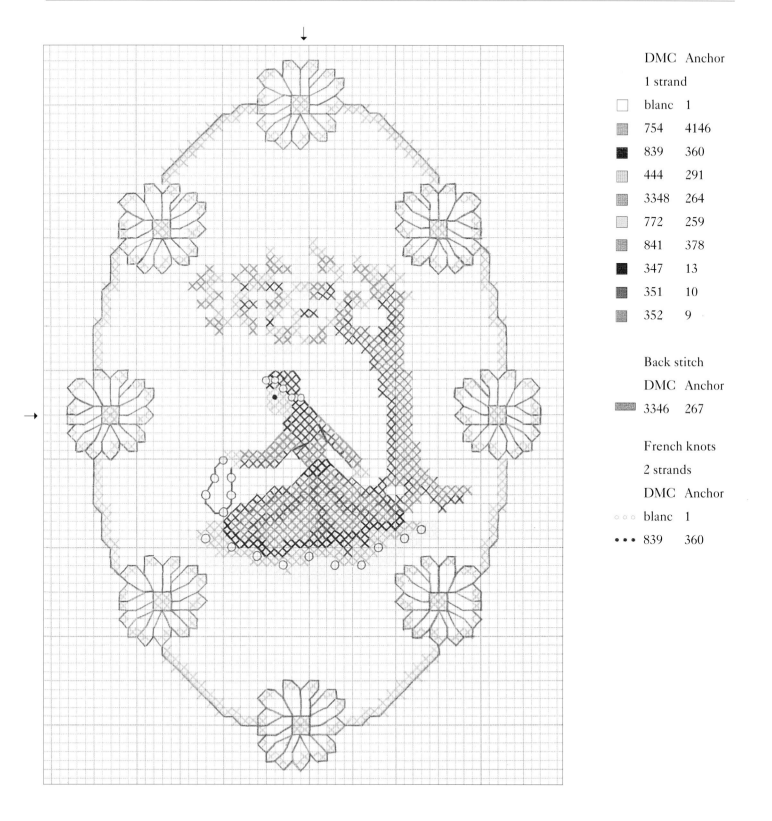

DMC   Anchor
1 strand
□   blanc   1
■   754   4146
■   839   360
■   444   291
■   3348   264
■   772   259
■   841   378
■   347   13
■   351   10
■   352   9

Back stitch
DMC   Anchor
■   3346   267

French knots
2 strands
DMC   Anchor
∘ ∘ ∘   blanc   1
• • •   839   360

Tulips

Reminiscent of the tulips on Dutch china, these stylized flowers are easy to stitch and quick to finish.

Measurements

The actual cross stitch design measures 4.8 x 7.2cm (1⅞ x 2⅞in)

Materials

- 13cm (5in) square of white 18-count Aida fabric
- One skein of stranded cotton in each colour listed in the key
- Size 26 tapestry needle
- Bright blue card with 8.3cm (3¼in) diameter circular opening

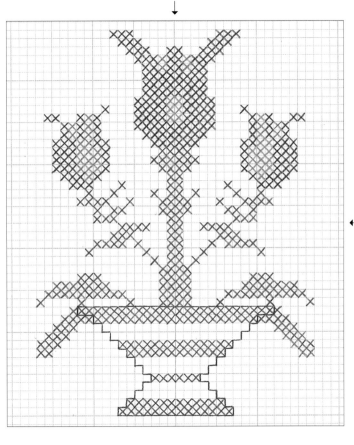

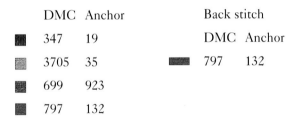

	DMC	Anchor		Back stitch	
				DMC	Anchor
■	347	19			
▨	3705	35		▬ 797	132
▨	699	923			
▨	797	132			

Sunflowers

For a special floral greeting, stitch these delicate sunflowers. Anyone receiving this card will be all sunny smiles.

Measurements
The actual cross stitch design measures 4.8 x 7cm (1⅞ x 2¾in)

Materials
- 13cm (5in) square of white 18-count Aida fabric
- One skein of stranded cotton in each colour listed in the key
- Size 26 tapestry needle
- Yellow card with oval opening measuring 5.2 x 8cm (2 x 3⅛in)

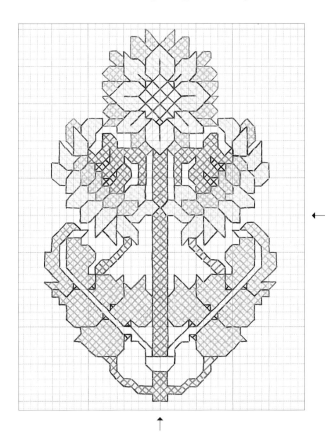

Note
If you use a larger count fabric, you can turn this lovely design into a bigger picture which could then be framed or worked as a front piece to a fabric bag.

DMC	Anchor		Back stitch		
1 strand			DMC	Anchor	
677	300		433	371	top flower outline,
726	295				inner detail of side flowers
991	189		3371	382	leaves, stems,
993	186				remainder of flowers
3371	382				

DESIGN SOURCES

Add a personal touch to your work by using these pages for inspiration. Once you've found something you like, select your own colours to suit the design you'd like to enhance. Or combine some of these ideas to create your own design.

abcdefghijklm
nopqrstuvwxyz

ABCDEƎGHICKℿ
NOPQRSTUVWXYƧ

abcdefghijklmnopqrstuvwxyz

ABCDEFGHIJKLMNOPQRSTUVWXYZ

abcdefghijklm
nopqrstuvwxyz

ABCDEƎGHIJKLM
NOPQRSTUVWXYZ

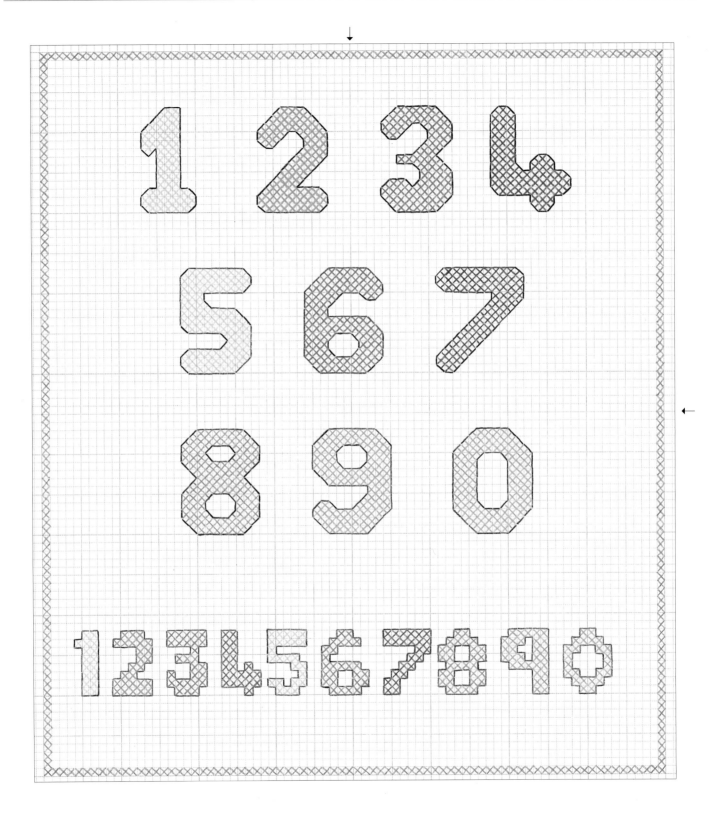

MATERIALS AND TECHNIQUES

In this section you will find a list of the materials you'll need, advice on different stitches, and a note on how to mount your cards.

Basic Equipment

Bobbins

Plastic or cardboard bobbins allow you to save unused strands of thread for re-use on a future project. Each will take a skein of thread and can be labelled with the thread make and number.

Card mounts

The card mounts used in this book show some of the wide range of sizes, shapes and colours available. All the cards used are known as double fold with aperture, meaning that each card is divided into three sections, with an aperture in the middle one. This enables you to mount your work with no raw edges showing and to have the back covered. Aperture shapes include rectangle, square, oval, circle and heart, and it is possible to obtain cards with an embossed, metallic or coloured line around the aperture. As with threads and fabrics, good embroidery shops should have a range of card mounts, but mail order is the best way to obtain the more unusual finishes or shapes (see page 111 for a suggested supplier).

Craft knife

A sharp knife is essential for obtaining a smooth, straight cut on card or paper. Replacement blades can be purchased separately.

Daylight simulation bulbs

These can be used in an anglepoise lamp for evening work, and for differentiating between similarly coloured threads.

Double-sided tape

This is good for mounting cards, being cleaner and easier to control than glue, which can be used if preferred.

Embroidery hoops and frames

The choice of a hoop or hand-held or floor-standing frame is a matter of personal preference. The use of either reduces distortion of your fabric, and it is worth having several in different sizes. It is a good idea to bind the inner hoop with tape or bias cut fabric to prevent it from marking your fabric.

Fabrics

The popularity of cross stitch has led to a huge increase in the variety of fabrics available. Colours range from white and pastels to black, in fancy weaves, which include lurex threads, or rustic-style fabrics, and there are tablecloths, tea towels and baby afghans which incorporate embroidery fabric panels. However, there are two basic types of fabric: blockweave and evenweave.

Blockweave The most popular blockweave is Aida. As the name implies, this is woven in blocks, and stitches are worked in every hole. Aida is available in a variety of counts, which refers to the number of holes (and therefore stitches) per inch. The most common counts are 11, 14 and 18. The higher the count, the smaller the finished design. As well as standard Aida, it is now possible to buy Aida Plus, which has been specially treated to prevent fraying and is therefore ideally suited for projects such as bookmarks, tree decorations and three-dimensional designs. Aida band is also available in a variety of widths and counts, and is ideal for bookmarks, cakebands and for stitching onto items such as tea towels, bedlinen and curtains.

Evenweave This fabric has the same numbers of threads across and down, and, like Aida, is available in a range of widths and stitch counts. The most popular is 27/28 holes per inch. On evenweave, stitches are usually worked into every other hole; thus a 27/28-count evenweave will produce the same finished design size as a 14-count Aida. It may be made of pure linen, linen and cotton mixes, or pure cotton. Whilst it can be more difficult to count on evenweave than on Aida, it does come into its own with designs using fractional stitches. It is also possible to work over just one thread to produce a half-size design.

Iron-on interfacing

Lightweight iron-on interfacing (Vilene) is useful when mounting cross stitch in commercially available boxes.

Magnifying glass

Hung around your neck, this can help on higher count fabrics. Magnifying aids are also available for placing on charts.

Needles

Tapestry needles are ideal for cross stitch: they are blunt, so do not damage fabric, and have a relatively large eye, making them easy to thread. Sizes 24 and 26 are the most commonly used, the latter being the finer and suitable for either 14 or 18 holes per inch fabric. Use size 24 for 14-count. If you intend to use beads, you may also need beading (or 'straw') needles. These are very fine, with an eye barely thicker than the shaft of the needle.

Pencil and pen

A pencil can be used for marking fabric but it may not always wash out, so be careful not to use it where it will show. Fabric markers are available which will wash out. Highlighter pens can be useful for marking off the worked sections of a chart.

Pins

Stainless steel pins are the best since they will not rust and mark your fabric. Other types, such as gold-plated and glass-headed, are also available.

Ruler

A metal ruler has the advantage over a bevelled plastic ruler of providing a flat edge when cutting card or paper.

Scissors

A large pair of dressmaking scissors is essential, and a cheaper pair for paper and card. (Do not be tempted to use dressmaking scissors for cutting card – you will blunt them.) Embroidery scissors have small, pointed blades which are ideal for cutting threads close to your work and for unpicking, but take care not to poke the blades into the fabric. Or use a pair of snips. They consist of two blades held together by a wire spring.

Tailor's chalk

Used for marking fabric, this will brush or wash away. It comes in a variety of colours to show up on different coloured fabrics.

Tape measure

It is best to choose a plastic-coated tape measure with both metric and imperial markings. It will not stretch out of shape in the way that a cloth one does and so it will give more accurate measurements.

Thimble

Use a thimble if you like. It's a matter of personal preference.

Threads

Again, the growth in the popularity of cross stitch has resulted in a broader range of threads. Most can be obtained from good embroidery shops, but mail order is also available.

Stranded cotton The projects in this book use stranded cotton, which comes in an excellent range of colours. The cotton has six strands which can be separated to produce the required number for a design. A design with 14 stitches per inch generally uses two strands, but a more intense effect can be obtained by using three strands. With 18 stitches per inch, two strands will produce a more solid effect, whereas one strand will give a lighter effect. In this book, there are usually two strands for cross stitch and one strand for back stitch and French knots unless otherwise stated.

Flower threads These are available in a narrower range of colours than stranded cottons and are single strands which should not be divided before using. They give a matt effect.

Marlitt This is lustrous and gives a sheen to your work. The colour range is more limited than that for stranded cottons.

Metallic threads These are available in a wide variety of colours and thicknesses. The finest is blending filament, which can be used on its own, single or double, or can be blended with one strand of stranded cotton. Two strands of blending filament is equivalent to two strands of embroidery cotton. The effect adds lustre and depth. Thicker metallic threads can be used singly as an alternative to stranded cotton – different thicknesses suit different gauges of fabric.

Tweezers

These are useful for removing threads when unpicking, and for removing the backing paper from double-sided tape.

Wadding (batting)

If you place a piece of lightweight wadding (2oz) behind your design when you mount it in a card, you will achieve a more professional, three-dimensional finish.

The Stitches

Whole cross stitch

Bring your threaded needle up in the lower left-hand corner of the block where you want your first stitch to be. The needle should then be passed back through the hole in the top right corner of the block. This will produce the lower half of your first stitch. To finish this stitch, pass the needle through the bottom right hole and then through the top left hole. If you are stitching a row, complete the lower halves first, returning along the row to complete each stitch. Left-handed stitchers may find it easier to reverse these instructions – i.e. read top right for bottom left, etc. The only essential rule to remember is that all your top stitches should lie in the same direction. If you follow this rule, you'll find that you produce neat, even work. Whole cross stitches are usually worked with two strands of cotton.

Half cross stitch

This is produced by only stitching the lower half of the stitch. It produces a lighter effect.

Three-quarter and quarter stitch

Stitch the lower half of the stitch as before, bringing the needle back up into position for the second half. Instead of inserting the needle into the usual hole, pass it through the centre of the half stitch already worked. If a quarter stitch of a second colour is required in the remaining space, bring your needle up in the vacant hole and insert it through the middle of the block to produce a cross. When deciding which colour you should use for the three-quarter and which to use for the quarter stitch, it is a good rule to do the three-quarter stitch in the foreground colour which you wish to be more dominant.

Back stitch

This is generally used for outlining the design, usually with one strand of cotton. First bring the needle up at the beginning of the back stitch line, then pass it down through the next hole along. Bring it up again one hole along, then go back and fill in the gap left. Continue in this way, following the lines as indicated on the chart.

French knots

French knots are easy to produce, but it is worth practising before stitching directly onto your work, to ensure you have developed the necessary rhythm. Use one strand for French knots unless otherwise stated. Bring your needle up through the fabric in the appropriate place. Wrap the thread around the needle (twice is sufficient for an average-sized knot) and push the needle back through the fabric close to where it came up. Do not push it through entirely at this stage. Pull the wrapped threads tightly against the fabric and around the needle. Push the needle through and gently tug to produce a neat French knot. Do not tug too hard or there is a danger the knot will disappear through to the other side.

There are six basic stitches you need to master for the cross stitch work in this book: cross stitch, three-quarter cross stitch, half cross stitch, back stitch, quarter stitch and French knots. These are pictured in the diagrams below.

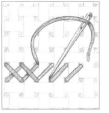
cross stitch

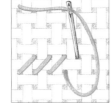
half cross stitch

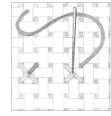
three-quarter stitch

quarter stitch

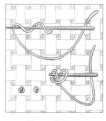
back stitch

French knot

Getting Ready to Stitch

Marking the centre

One of the beauties of cross stitch is the small amount of preparatory work necessary before starting to stitch. The first task is to cut your fabric to the recommended size and find its centre by folding it in half both vertically and horizontally. Crease along these lines lightly and open out your fabric. You can use either these crease lines to indicate the centre or tack along them for a more permanent mark, removing the tacking when the cross stitch is complete. On small projects such as cards, tacking is perhaps not necessary. Next, find the centre of the chart by counting the maximum number of its squares both vertically and horizontally. Divide both by two, and count the resulting number of squares down and across. It is generally recommended that you start stitching in the centre of your fabric since this ensures the design will fit. In this book, the chart centres have been marked for you with arrows at the side and top of the charts.

Following the charts

Cross stitch charts use symbols, colours or a combination of both to indicate which thread is used where. The accompanying key shows the meaning of the symbols or colours. Each box on the chart represents one block of fabric. Consequently a box with one symbol in it means that one whole cross stitch should be made using the appropriate thread colour in that position. A box with two symbols in opposing corners means that a three-quarter stitch and a quarter stitch are required in this position. A box with just one symbol in a corner shows that a single three-quarter stitch is needed. If liked, worked stitches can be marked off with a highlighter pen to help keep your place. This can be particularly useful on a large, complicated chart.

Starting to stitch

You are now ready to start stitching. Refer to the chart and its accompanying key to identify your first thread colour. Cut a length and separate the required number of strands. There are several ways to start stitching, but the following two are easy and practical.

• Thread the required number of strands in the normal way, then insert the needle through the back of the work in the right place. Leave a 2.5cm (1in) length at the back and sew over it with your first stitches.

• If the design calls for an even number of strands, the following method of casting on leaves no loose ends. Remove one strand, fold it in half and thread the two cut ends through your needle. Bring the needle up from the back of the fabric, make your first half cross stitch and pass the needle through the loop of the doubled-over thread. Pull gently to tighten.

Stitching your design

1 Find the centre of your chart and the centre of your fabric. Start stitching from the middle of your work.

2 Using one or two strands of cotton as specified, work the cross stitch, working all the stitches in each colour before moving on to the next. Unless specified, all cross stitch designs in this book use two strands of cotton for the cross stitch and one strand for back stitch and French knots.

3 Finish by working all the back stitch and French knots.

To finish stitching

Threads should be finished off by passing them underneath several stitches on the back of your work and trimming them carefully. Most threads nowadays are colourfast and your work can therefore be washed. Use lukewarm water and gently hand-wash. Do not wring. If any bleeding of colours does occur, keep rinsing until the water is clear. Then place your embroidery in a clean white towel, roll it up, and squeeze gently. This will remove excess water. Unroll, lay it face down on a clean, dry towel, and cover with a dry cloth. Finally, press lightly with a medium-heat iron until completely dry. You can then mount your work.

Mounting the Cards

You will need:

• card with suitable aperture
• stitched piece
• double-sided tape
• 2oz wadding (batting)
• all-purpose scissors
• pencil
• tweezers

1 Fold the card along the scored foldlines if this has not already been done. Open it out and place the card right-side down on a piece of wadding. Draw carefully around the aperture onto the wadding with a pencil, taking care not to mark the mount. Lift the card off and cut along the pencil line.

2 Place the opened card right-side down on a clean surface. Cut some pieces of double-sided tape and stick them all around the aperture. Then remove the backing paper from the tape, using tweezers to lift the backing paper if you have difficulty.

3 Place the embroidery right-side up on your work surface and gradually lower the card mount onto it, right-side up. Ensure your design is straight and central in the aperture. When you are happy with the positioning, press down carefully to stick your embroidery to the tape. Ensure that the embroidery remains taut.

4 Turn the card over. Place your wadding over the back of your cross stitch and secure with tape.

5 Stick double-sided tape to the side of the card which will cover the back of the embroidery. This is the left-hand panel on a side-opening card and the top panel on a bottom-opening card. Remove backing paper and press card shut firmly. With your finger, rub along the edges of the card and around the aperture to ensure adhesion.

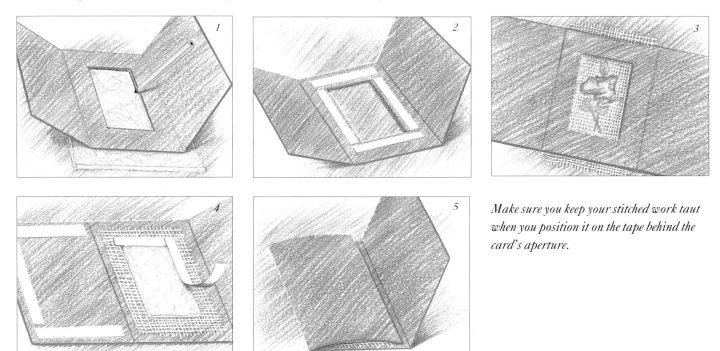

Make sure you keep your stitched work taut when you position it on the tape behind the card's aperture.

Suppliers

UK

Coats Crafts UK
PO Box 22, The Lingfield Estate
McMullen Road
Darlington
County Durham DL1 1YQ
Tel : 01325 394394
*(Suppliers of embroidery fabrics, Anchor
threads and Kreinik metallic threads)*

Craft Creations Ltd
Units 1-7
Harper's Yard
Ruskin Road
Tottenham
London N17 8QA
Tel : 0181 885 2655
Fax : 0181 808 0746
*(Suppliers of card mounts, card, paper,
packaging, picture mounts, etc. Orders
accepted from abroad)*

DMC Creative World
Pullman Road
Wigston
Leicester
Leicestershire   E18 2DY

USA

The DMC Corporation
Port Kearny
Building 10
South Kearny
New Jersey 070032

Coats and Clark
Greenville
South Carolina
(Anchor threads)

Joan Toggit Ltd
2 Riverview Drive
Somerset
New Jersey 08873
(Zweigart fabrics)

AUSTRALIA AND
NEW ZEALAND

DMC
51-61 Carrington Road
Marrickville
New South Wales 2204

Warnaar Trading Co Ltd
376 Ferry Road
PO Box 19567
Christchurch
(DMC threads and Zweigart fabrics)

Coats Patons Crafts
Mulgrave 3170
Australia
(Anchor threads)

SOUTH AFRICA

SATC
43 Somerset Road
PO Box 3868
Capetown 800
(DMC threads)

Brasch Hobby
10 Loveday Street
PO Box 6405
Johannesburg 2000
(Zweigart fabrics)

NEEDLE PRODUCTS
All DMC and Anchor threads and Zweigart fabrics used in this book are available from the relevant stockists given below and many other needlecraft outlets the world over. The addresses given are the head offices or agents – contact them for advice on local availability of threads. Good haberdasheries should also supply other products, including embroidery hoops, cards, needles, scissors etc.

Index

Aida fabric 106
alphabets 98-101
Animal Sampler 12-13
Arum Lilies 80-1

back stitch 108
Bear Repeat 11
birthday cards 18-29
birth cards 8-17
blockweave fabric 106
Bluebells 83
border designs 94-7
Boy's 18th or 21st (Key) 26
Boy's 18th or 21st (Motorbike) 24-5

centre, marking 109
charts, following 109
Christmas cards 62-73
Children's Toys 72-3
cross stitch
  basic stitches 108
  technique 109

Daisies 84-5
design source charts 90-103

Driving Test 48-9
Easter Chick 57
Easter Cross 58
Engagement Congratulations 32
engagement and wedding cards 30-39
equipment 106-7
Exams 46

fabric 106
Father's Day 60-61
Fireplace and Stockings 71
floral greetings 74-87
flower threads 107
Forget-me-nots 78
frames 106
French knot 108

Get Well Soon 51
Girl's 18th Birthday (Key) 22
Girl's 18th or 21st (Wild Rose) 23
Good Luck 42
good luck cards 40-51

Happy New Year 54

Holly and Ivy 67
Honeysuckle 79
hoops 106
Little Boy's 1st Birthday 21
Little Girl's 1st Birthday 20

Man's 70th/80th/90th Birthday 27
marlitt 107
metallic threads 107
Moses Basket 10
Mother's Day 59
mounts 106
  mounting a card 110

needles 107
New Home 44-5
New Job 43
New Year Chimney Sweep 55
numbers 102-3

Poinsettia 66
Poppies 82

Robin 68-9
Roses 76-77

Santa 64-5
scissors 107
Silver Anniversary 38-39
special occasion cards 52-61
stitches 108
Stork and Baby 14-15
stranded cotton 107
Sunflowers 87

tassel, making a 46
threads 107
Toy Sampler 16-17
Travel or Moving Abroad 47
Tulips 86
Valentine's Day 56
Visit to Hospital 50

wadding 107
washing 109
Wedding Congratulations 33
Wedding Congratulations and Place Card 34-5
Wedding Sampler 36-7
Winter Scene 70
Woman's 70th/80th/90th Birthday 28-9

ACKNOWLEDGEMENTS

The authors would like to thank the following designers for use of their designs:

LYNDA BURGESS – 18/21 flower/key, 18/21 wild rose, forget-me-nots, poppies;

LESLEY GRANT – Moses basket, 18/21 motorbike, 70/80/90 female, exams, New Year chimney sweep, Father's day (man and dog in pub), winter scene, sunflower, wedding doves (card and tag);

LUCIE HEATON – animal sampler, bear repeat, toy sampler, New Year champagne;

STEVEN JENKINS – 18/21 football, 70/80/90 male, Mother's day bouquet, holly and ivy;

PENELOPE RANDALL – boy's 1st birthday, girl's 1st birthday, new job, travel, Santa;

JANE RIMMER – good luck, driving test (car), Easter chick, robin;

JULIA TIDMARSH – stork (card and tag), engagement congratulations, new home, Easter cross, Valentine's day, poinsettia, fireplace with stockings, honeysuckle, daisies;

SUE WHITING – bride and groom, silver anniversary, arum liles, bluebells, tulips;

LYNDA WHITTLE – rabbit in hospital bed, get well soon flower basket, wedding sampler, presents with doll/teddy, roses.

Special thanks also to Coats Crafts UK and to Craft Creations Ltd for providing materials for the cards.